Fairytale
Quilts
& Embroidery

FAIRYTALE QUILTS & EMBROIDERY

GAIL HARKER

MEREHURST

LONDON

DEDICATION

This book is dedicated to my husband and partner, Don, who helped me
at every stage of the process, and to all my children – Don, Christie,
Michael, Heather, Adam and Bobbi.

Published 1992 by Merehurst Limited
Ferry House
51–57 Lacy Road
Putney
London SW15 1PR

Reprinted 1994 (twice)

© Copyright 1992 Merehurst Limited
ISBN 1 85391 145 3 (Cased)
ISBN 1 85391 384 7 (Paperback)

A catalogue record for this book is available from the British Library.

Project Editor: Polly Boyd
Edited by Diana Brinton
Designed by Bill Mason
Photography by Stewart Grant except pages 7 (Metropolitan Museum of
Art); 31 (top), 40–41, 49, 51 (right), 54 (right), 61, 73 (left) (Marie-
Louise Avery); 74–75, 85, 88 (left), 99 (Di Lewis)
Illustrations by Lindsay Blow except pages 20–23 (Lorna Townsend);
109 (Barbara and Roy Hirst)
Typesetting by Maron Graphics Limited
Colour separation by Fotographics Limited, London – Hong Kong
Printed in China

*Merehurst Limited is the leading publisher of craft books and has an excellent
range of titles to suit all levels. Please send to the address above for
our free catalogue, stating the title of this book.*

CONTENTS

INTRODUCTION

'Tell me a story!' cries the child, and out of the fertile imaginations of
ancient story tellers come the tales of fancy that have captured the
imaginations of succeeding generations, and still retain powerful appeal.
Why? Perhaps it is because these oft-told tales contain the qualities of
humanity, evoke laughter, tears, and sentiment.

F airy stories hark back to the oral traditions of all societies, when tales of morality or life-lessons were conveyed around the camp fire or hearth. The classic story of Cinderella, for instance, is found throughout Europe in more than 500 variations, with a Chinese version on the theme going back to the 9th century AD.

Aladdin and the Magic Lamp, Rumpelstiltskin, Hansel and Gretel – however long it may be since we heard a particular tale, the mere mention of a story that once moved us to delight will often conjure up a vivid mental picture from a childhood story book.

This book is dedicated to the retelling of those tales, myths and legends, to the creation of new stories, and to finding an artistic and personal expression of these imaginings – through fabrics and threads. The new works will range from embroidered panels and pictorial representations to functional bed quilts and quilted hangings. We will also look at the construction of embroidered fairy tale books, in which an entire story may be unfolded through a series of illustrated pages.

In this book, the wide range of techniques that have been used by successful textile artists in their own interpretation of fairy tales will be explored and explained. We will de-mystify design, fabric dyeing, stitches, colour and construction methods, and examine a whole range of embroidery and quilting techniques, some of which are fully explained in step-by-step procedures.

A familiarity with fabrics and threads is a worthwhile endeavour to pursue. It can be imperative to know how various fabrics will react under hand or machine stitches, how they will dye, how stiff or limp they may be, or even whether or not they are washable or dry-cleanable. For these reasons, fabrics and threads will be explored in various sections of the book wherever appropriate.

An important part of the creative process is to test and experiment with threads, fabrics and techniques. Not only will tests and experiments save problems, but they also lead the way to new methods of working, perhaps some that have never been tried before. The creative worker will have dozens of such sample pieces for reference, and hopefully the ideas and techniques shown here will inspire you to creative experiments of your own.

It is my hope that with every page you turn, you will find your imagination stirred by the finished embroideries and quilts, and the details of the techniques used in their creation. I hope the information will fill you with self confidence in your ability to tackle your own dream.

An illustration from a book by B. V. Zvorykin introducing the story of the firebird. Courtesy of the Metropolitan Museum of Art, Gift of Thomas H. Guinzburg, The Viking Press, 1979.

L'OISEAU DE FEU

ans un certain royaume d'autrefois, dans un certain empire, habitait jadis le roi Visslaff ✳ Andronovitch. Chez lui étaient trois fils tsarévitches : le pre ✳ mier, le tsarévitch Dimitri ; un autre, le tsarévitch Vassili, et le troisième, le tsarévitch Ivan. Chez ce roi, était un jardin tellement magnifique que ; ✳ dans aucun royaume, il n'y en avait de meil-

CHAPTER I

GETTING STARTED

You do not need to be an accomplished artist to design your own fairy tale
work of art – there are many simple ways of transferring your own special
inspiration to paper and then to a creation of fabric and thread.

First, read your chosen tale several times – you will be surprised how often additional readings will highlight the little nuances that can flesh out a design concept. Before attempting to sketch this image, write down descriptive passages of the scene your imagination has created out of the text. Close your eyes, see the picture, then try to describe what you 'see' in short phrases or words.

Now try to organize this image on paper. Do not get too detailed at first; what is needed is a pleasing general layout, indicating the placement of figures, buildings, and any other items of special interest. Use stick figures, rectangles, triangles, or any other roughly equivalent shape.

Next, you can use another trick out of the bag of the professional artist – the catalogue of 'clip art'. Commercial artists have books full of small drawings of animals, people, buildings and so on. These may be traced, enlarged, reduced or changed to suit the need. You might make your own collection from brochures, magazines, travel literature, and news-paper advertising, also including old prints and art works of all kinds.

Look through your collection to find forms and shapes to fit your layout. Remember, they may be reversed, enlarged, or reduced on a photocopier. Armed with this collection of odds and ends, you can create a fairly good layout, with probably more detail than is needed. Just paste the forms down in the positions you have already identified, creating a collage. One note of caution – be aware of the per-spective of the various pieces that are to be fitted together.

Over your collage, lay a piece of tracing paper and trace the basic shapes and forms in the amount of detail suited to the needlework technique that you intend to use. The greatest amount of detail should be in the foreground.

Clothing may be drawn over the top of any figures you may have traced from the collage. Libraries and museums are a good source of histor-ical information for clothing and other details.

An alternative method of establishing a basic design is to find a book containing old illustrations of your favourite fairy tale. Select an illustration that you feel is particularly exceptional or portrays the essence of the tale you wish to project.

Many fairy tale books will have illustrations or pages enclosed in borders. Take a good look at these, and decide whether they are important to the design and the atmosphere of the picture. Also take note of the colours used in the artwork, and the feeling you may sense from them. Look at the costume of the characters – does it suggest a period of time or a place? How much detail is there in the background? Does it set the scene?

You may decide that the piece of work will only be a small portion of the original scene. Try to simplify the shapes and designs, keeping in mind the limitations of the technique to be used.

Build your own inspirational still life by placing household treasures and fabrics in a grouping. The arrangement might lead to new ideas and, perhaps, suggest a setting for your personal fairy tale. The pleated silk fabric behind the doll was dyed by Vivien Prideaux.

SCALE AND PROPORTION

B efore embarking on a fairy tale project, it is important to establish its size and purpose. If the project is to be a bed quilt, the size of the bed must be known. If a fairy tale book is to be made, what will the page dimensions be? The design may need to be enlarged or reduced, and the proportion of width to height must be determined.

Wherever possible, for pieces of up to about a square metre (yard), it is much easier to draw the design on paper to the exact size of the finished piece. If your embroidery is very small, however, it may be desirable to make the design larger than the finished piece. It is very difficult to work on an extremely small design, and for this reason, a postage stamp, for example, is designed very much larger and then reduced to the finished size. Alternatively, designs for very large pieces would be difficult to handle if they were drawn at full size.

SCALE

Scale refers to the ratio to which the design may require enlargement or reduction. For instance, if the ratio is 1:1, this means that the design is the same size as the finished piece; a 1:5 ratio means that the piece is five times as large as the working design. So 5cm (2in) on the original will be equal to 25cm (10in) on the enlargement. Reduction is indicated in the same way, but with the larger number first, so 5:1 is a reduction to 1/5th of the original size; 25cm (10in) on the original will therefore be equal to 5cm (2in) on the reduction.

Much detail can be lost through reduction; as designs are enlarged, on the other hand, they can look very sparse. It is important, therefore, to project the design to its actual size before proceeding with the project.

PHOTOCOPIER ENLARGEMENT

There are a number of practical ways to enlarge designs. One of the easiest is through the use of a photocopier. Most office photocopiers are capable of enlargements, and many will make copies up to A3 size (11¾ × 16½in). If the finished design is no larger than the largest size of paper available on the machine, this can prove an easily accomplished enlarging method. If the largest paper available on the photocopier is smaller than the required finished design size, the latter will need to be enlarged in sections, allowing several sheets to be pieced together to achieve the correct size. Most of the larger machines will be capable of enlargement or reduction to a percentage of the actual size of the original.

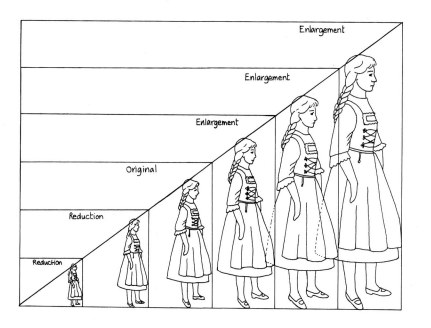

To enlarge a design, draw a diagonal line across the original and place it over a larger sheet of paper. Using a straight edge, continue the diagonal line across the new paper. Next, draw a horizontal line crossing the diagonal at the desired width. At the point where the horizontal line crosses the diagonal, draw a vertical line to the bottom of the paper. The new paper will now be in perfect proportion to the original. Reverse the process to reduce a design.

OTHER METHODS

Overhead projectors If you have access to one of these, it can be used enlarge designs. The original design may be drawn, painted, or traced on a transparency. This can then be projected to the fabric (or whatever medium you are using). Fasten the fabric to a wall. Adjust the position of the overhead projector so that the projected image is the desired size, then trace the image directly on the fabric.

Slide projectors The 35mm camera and slide projector can be handy devices for any artist. They are especially convenient for enlarging. First, take a slide photo of the design or use an existing slide. Simply attach the fabric (or other medium) to a wall and project the design onto it. To prevent distortion of the image, position the projector to the exact height of the centre of the fabric. This will keep the projector level and the beam will be centred on the fabric. By moving the projector nearer to or further from the fabric, or by using a zoom lens, you can achieve the exact size required. The design can then be traced directly onto paper or the fabric.

Computer scanners Some computer scanners will enlarge designs by up to 400 per cent. These will be visible on the computer display monitor and can be printed out in sections. Use these as you would the photocopier grid enlargements.

PROPORTION

Often, one is faced with trying to use a design that is not the same shape as is required for the piece of work. For instance, a square design does not lend itself to a rectangular quilt. In this case, the object is to make the length and sides of the artwork fit the length and sides of the finished work. It is obvious that if one is drawing an original design, it should be done with these proportions in mind. If you are using a design of different proportions from those of the finished work, you must decide which parts of the design are to be either cropped or eliminated from the finished piece.

The proportions are, again, a ratio of width to length: a quilt 1.8m (6ft) long by 90cm (3ft) wide would have the proportion of 2:1 or 180 (6) divided

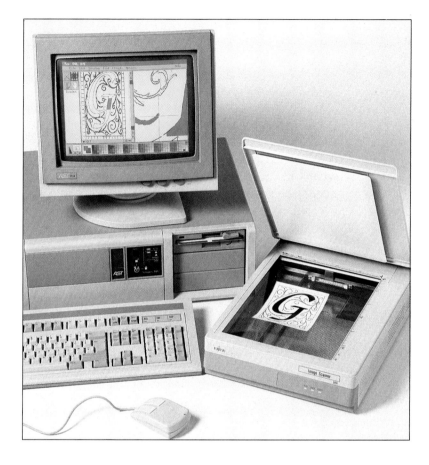

The illuminated letter design was scanned and transferred to the graphics programme. The image could then be scaled to almost any size. For a very large work, such as a quilt with a large central monogram, the design could be divided by a grid and each portion printed on a letter-sized page. The repeated letter could be used in a border design or as a first letter on a fairy tale book page.

by 90 (3). The original design could be any size, but to fit the shape it should be twice as long as it is wide. Any proportion can be worked out by dividing one side by the other.

Another method is to draw a diagonal line to opposite corners of the finished shape. Any horizontal line drawn to the diagonal and intersected by a vertical line drawn to that intersection creates a shape that is proportional to the other, larger or smaller.

COMPUTER GRAPHICS FOR NEEDLEWORKERS

I t is important for us, as needleworkers, to be able to use the most up-to-date designing tools available, and the computer is a tool we will all be using more and more as time progresses. For the purpose of needlework design, a computer must be equipped with a 'graphics processing board'. Most current computers are supplied with these boards installed. There are a few other devices that can be added at reasonable cost and will radically extend the usefulness of your computer.

DRAWING AND DESIGNING TOOLS

Many computer graphics processing programmes – known as graphics software – are readily available in the marketplace.

The actual computing knowledge demanded of the artist is minimal. Graphics programmes will normally have a wide variety of the 'clip art' already discussed. These symbols are merely transferred from a library held in the computer and added to the work being developed. They can be moved about the drawing, enlarged, reduced, mirrored, inverted, and so on. If you are working in colour, a wide variety of colour schemes is available and can be changed with a keystroke.

Drawings can be made and images manipulated with a hand-held pointing device, universally called a 'mouse'.

PRINTERS

Your existing printer is probably suitable for most uses. If you wish to produce your designs to a high definition, you could use a laser printer, which works like a photocopier. If these are not available at home, most offices will have them. The graphics programme, working with the graphics board, composes your designs in a special language understood by the printer and produces prints resembling photocopies.

There are printers that will print in colour at reasonable cost. The dot matrix, or impact printers, work in a similar way to a typewriter. As with the laser printers, the graphics programme will automatically organize your artwork for the printer.

PRINTING ON FABRIC

Printers will print directly on fabrics of medium to heavy weight and on most interfacings, sometimes up to 33 cm × 45 cm (13 in × 18 in) in size. Laser printers require a fairly stiff fabric. Inserting fabric into a printer may require a little manipulation, but this capability opens a whole new vista for needleworkers. Full-colour layouts can be produced for canvaswork (needlepoint), cross stitch, machine or

LEFT *The ideal computer graphics set up would include (clockwise from top left) colour graphics computer (AST Premium/386C); dot matrix colour printer (Fujitsu DL1100); laser printer (Fujitsu RX7100PS) and scanner (Fujitsu Image Scanner 3191), plus a digitizing tablet (Hitachi Puma-S1).*

RIGHT *The laser printer has printed the design on interfacing. A full-colour border design is printed on stiffened fabric with a dot matrix printer.*

BELOW RIGHT *The left side of the display shows drawing and painting tools, including pencil, spray painter, a tool to fill areas with colour or pattern, an eraser, a paintbrush, and a hand to move pieces around the screen. At the bottom is one of many colour palettes available (PC Paintbrush IV Plus, trademark of ZSoft Corporation).*

traditional embroideries. Quilting patterns and templates can be produced to accurate dimensions. Very large patterns and designs can be reproduced by printing and assembling the elements of a grid. Repeating border patterns of great diversity can be produced in minutes.

Other useful printers for the needleworker use a print head composed of tiny ink jets that squirt minute dots of ink on paper or fabric. These will produce both black and white, and full-colour prints, and are usually brighter and more intense in colour than dot matrix printers.

EXTRAS

Two other items of equipment can be recommended. One of these is a special drawing board for computers. Universally used by graphics artists, these are called 'digitizing tablets'. A mouse-like pointer or pencil-like stylus is used to draw on the tablet, and the drawing appears on the screen of the computer display monitor as you draw on the tablet. With this drawing board, you can create designs and patterns as if you were drawing them in your sketch pad.

The other device I would suggest for the serious needlework designer is a 'scanner'. This works exactly like a photocopier, but it transfers the image to your graphics programme. Hand-held scanners, about 10cm (4in) across, are very low-cost units. These are simply rolled across the photograph or drawing, which is automatically transferred to the graphics programme. Colour scanners are available, but are very costly. Even the black-and-white ones, however, are an invaluable tool for lifting images and inserting them into a design. With the scanner, clip art is at your finger tips, and from any source.

CARTOONS

T he cartoon, which is drawn on paper, is the design or study to be transferred to the medium selected for the fairy tale. A familiarity with the strengths and limitations of various techniques will often dictate the degree of detail and scale that should be incorporated in the cartoon. Fine details, such as noses, or fingers, are quite feasible with some techniques, but difficult with others.

Trace your cartoon from a favourite illustration or from your own design. Do not be too impatient, but try a range of different ideas. I normally sketch a number of designs and end up with a final piece incorporating elements from each. Keep the design simplified, without too much detail at this stage. If your cartoon is not made to the size of the finished piece, try enlarging or reducing it to its actual size to get a better idea of the finished piece.

COLOUR

Your observation of fairy tale illustrations should offer suggestions as to the mood you wish to set in your own work. Develop a colour scheme and apply the selected colours to the cartoon. The palette of threads and fabric dyes has never before offered a greater variety, so if you are going to make good use of your options, add colour to the cartoon.

When applying colour to your cartoon, use any medium that is readily at hand. Try using children's wax crayons to fill in areas; a gouache or water colour wash applied over the crayons will create a fairy-like iridescence, due to the water-repelling nature of the wax. There are iridescent and metallic crayons, felt-tip pens and markers, pastels, and water-soluble pencils that turn into water colours when moistened with a brush.

Often the use of different types of media will spark off ideas suggesting a particular needleworking technique. After applying colour, the cartoon can be enlarged or reduced to actual size using a colour photocopier.

What is the benefit of all this development on paper when you are going to be working with fabric and threads? The simple answer is that the more you think about your design, the figures and other elements in it, and the colours to be used, the more intimately you will know it.

Be absolutely daring with colour, and experiment, experiment, experiment! Go darker or lighter than you would ordinarily do. Break the rules, as mother nature does. Mix pinks and reds, or blues and greens – the results can be startlingly beautiful.

TEXTURES

Some stitchery techniques have great texture, so try to develop your cartoon to indicate this. Select several papers of different colours (these could be sprayed with aerosol enamels, cut from magazines, or coloured papers). Starting with a line drawing or photocopy of the design, tear off very small pieces of coloured paper and paste them to spaces on the

FAR LEFT *Scheherazade's Tales of* One Thousand and One Nights *inspired Janet Edmonds to work on a paper collage as a design or cartoon on this theme. She collected papers of all colours; tore them into small bits, and glued them to a background paper. As the paper pieces were progressively built up, Janet added colour with pastels and water-soluble paints, intensifying some colours and filling in gaps and cracks in the collage.*

LEFT *Needlework designers have need of the usual tools of the artist, and here are some that are available in the market place. Caran D'Ache water-soluble pencils and crayons are useful for colouring cartoons. Raphael make a range of artists' brushes, and their sponge brushes are good for laying on washes of colour or dye. In addition to dyes and fabric paints, Pebeo also supply a range of inks and gouaches.*

design. Build up shadows with darker papers and highlights with lighter colours. Fill in any gaps with coloured pencils. The same effect may be translated to the needlework by using a bonded fabric (transfer fusing web) to attach similar pieces of fabric to the background. Fabric pens may be used to fill in any remaining spaces.

THE BACKGROUND

If your design is centred around one or two subjects, the background could be kept very simple. Excitement may be added through the application of complementary or contrasting colours. If your back-ground includes trees or forests, paint the whole background with gouache, poster paint, or ink. While it is still wet, lay a sheet of plastic film over the top. Let it dry. When the plastic is removed, it will leave an eerie impression of mysterious woods.

Swirls of colour can be created by dropping ink or paint on a wetted paper. Aerosol spray enamels, the kind used for automobile touch-up, can be sprayed on the background. (*Caution: always spray in a well-ventilated room or out of doors.*) These enamels may also be lightly sprayed on fabric – a heavy application can make the fabric very stiff.

INSPIRATION FROM FABRIC AND THREADS

A vast array of specialist fabrics and threads is available to the quilter and embroiderer. Fabrics will vary from pure cotton for the quilters, to delicate organzas and organdies, silks of all weights, and medium to heavy cotton for the machine embroiderer, and a variety of canvases for needlepoint. Many fabrics are devised for purposes other than embroidery, but embroiderers and quilters enjoy a long history of using and adapting whichever is at hand. If specific materials are not readily available, try substitutes.

Do not dismiss any unusual finds of fabric and thread, therefore. Interfacings, muslins, lace, and even hand-made papers – anything through which you can pass a needle – are suitable for the embroiderer.

FABRICS

The most commonly used and traditional fabric for patchwork quilting is pure cotton. Some manufacturers dye their cottons in a multitude of shades and tones of colours in response to the demands of quilters. Many beautiful quilts use the subtle tonal changes in colour to create designs, and even though fabric may have been pre-dyed, that does not preclude printing over the colour.

Take into account the end use of your work. Will it require washing or dry-cleaning, or will it be a wall hanging or some other non-functional item that will not require rigorous cleaning? Some embroiderers express a preference for blends of polyester and cotton. Others, especially those who do appliqué, find that pure cotton turns more easily at the edges and is easier to stitch by hand. The polyester-cotton blends are not, generally, satisfactory for machine embroidery. The fabric is difficult to machine embroider and will not bear the weight of heavy stitching. If a wide range of fabrics is not readily available, refer to the section on painting fabrics. Bleached and unbleached sheeting may be dyed and painted with fabric paints in an unlimited range of colour and tones.

THREADS

Dressmakers' threads are the ones most often displayed in sewing shops, but they are quite different from machine embroidery threads. Threads manufactured specifically for machine embroidery lack the strength and high twist of general sewing threads. As a result, they are softer and have a tendency to spread and cover a larger area with fewer passes of the needle. Machine embroidery threads will appear more lustrous and decorative, but it is not good practice to use them to sew seams. They are best for free machining, appliqué, needlelace, and machine quilting.

The numbering system used to designate thread sizes is not universal. General sewing threads are usually size 50, though a number may not be indicated; size 50 machine embroidery threads are very fine in comparison. A size 40 general sewing thread will be quite coarse and will probably clog the machine if used for machine embroidery; a machine embroidery thread numbered size 40 will be a fairly fine thread.

Hand quilters, too, have a range of threads specifically manufactured for their craft. These threads are specially prepared, both to allow easy passage through fabric and batting, and for strength. Some of these may not be numbered with a size. Quilters, however, will often use other types of thread. Before the advent of coated threads, quilters would pass the thread through a block of beeswax, and this can still be done if required. If quilting is applied to a decorative piece of work that does not require much washing or dry-cleaning, machine embroidery threads may be used.

A vast range of cotton fabrics, as well as some synthetics with their sparkling sheens, are now available to inspire needleworkers. The threads shown here include Madeira machine embroidery threads, rayon, Tanné cotton, metallics, Gütermann sewing silks, polyesters, and cotton machine embroidery threads.

BORDERS

F rom the time man first began making his own implements and tools, he sought to make them more beautiful. By applying edge decorations to pottery, the ancient Chinese turned mundane implements into works of art. Chinese potters began using geometric shapes to decorate their wares some 5,000 years ago. The decoration took on spiritual connotations with the acceptance of standard symbols – the dragon represented the emperor, for example, while the bamboo symbolized a scholarly spirit, bending under strain, but never broken.

For me, a well-designed and colour-coordinated border is the crowning glory of a well-executed piece of work, giving the finishing touch to a piece of needlework or a quilt, just as the right mount and frame complete a picture.

Borders may be as narrow or as wide as desired. Some are as much as a quarter of the width of the panel. A very wide border could be composed of design elements taken from the main story; these could be arranged in a repeating pattern or there might be a whole series of individual story-related designs or figures. Patterns may be divided by fabric strips to give a multi-banded effect. Plan the bands so that they all have a different width. As few as two or three strips could be used, or up to 20 or more.

ABOVE The Dream of Maxen *by Denise Harrison, a framed panel, was inspired by a tale from* The Mabinogion, *a collection of tales from the oral traditions of Wales. The main panel is hand quilted on painted silk; the borders incorporate free machine embroidery with hand and machine couching. Size 26in × 33cm (10in × 13in).*

CHOOSING A STYLE

When you are choosing a theme for your border, it is well worth looking at the various styles of the past. Old fairy tale books, in which the illustrations are often surrounded and complemented by beautiful borders, can be a useful source of inspiration, but there are other possibilities and traditions, some of which the fairy tale illustrators themselves used.

Think of art nouveau pictures in which flower garlands flow out of the central picture and around the edges, forming a beautiful entwining border. Similarly, the illuminators of medieval manuscripts often devoted as much care and artistic inspiration

to their framing borders as to the central theme. Ancient tapestry artists used to enhance the main theme with borders.

In all these cases, it is important to note that the borders were designed not as an afterthought, but as an integral part of the design.

FINDING A SYMBOL

Many of the traditional design motifs for borders are thousands of years old. That longevity can in part be attributed to their simplicity and consequent versatility. Geometric shapes, whorls, circles, chevrons, sawteeth, squared spirals, and volutes (the scroll-like

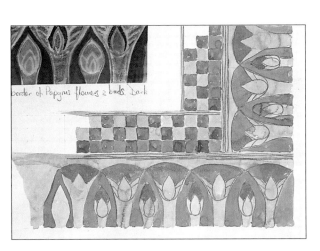

ABOVE AND RIGHT *The Egyptian Story, by Angela Howard, is a large floor cushion featuring the ancient motif of the squared spiral, sometimes known as log cabin. Size: 80 cm (32 in) square.*

The artist experimented with several design ideas on paper. Turning corners can present problems, but Angela has achieved this to perfection.

spirals on Ionic capitals), in repeating patterns, have been used by artists for hundreds, even thousands of years. By the time of the 3rd century BC, zigzags, lozenges, scallops, and quatrefoils (four-petalled flowers) had come into general usage as border designs.

The ancient Egyptians evolved patterns incorporating papyrus, palms, bundles of flowering reeds, and lotus blossoms. They also developed a standard for the rendering of the human figure that was used for many centuries until the reign of Akhnaton. This liberal pharaoh, who wished to be depicted as he appeared, relieved contemporary Egyptian artists

of their traditional formalities and constraints.

The Egyptians devised a measure of 18 equally-spaced lines to proportion the figure. For the head, beginning at the hairline to the base of the neck, two lines were allowed. Head to knees was allocated 10 lines, with the remaining six from knees to sole. An extra line was allowed above the head for hair. The figures were further standardized, with heads always in profile, a triangular body form, arms facing front, and legs in profile. All figures were required to be so drawn. Any border that incorporates a repeating pattern of such figures, designed to those proportions, will take on an ancient Egyptian air.

CREATING A BORDER PATTERN

N ew patterns are developed every day, and they can easily be designed to reflect individual interests. You might, for example, create your own space-age fairy tale for a child who is captivated by space travel. Space-age borders could be composed of simplified rockets, space stations, astronauts, and so on, in repeating sequences.

The point to be remembered is that any shape or doodle can be used in a repeating pattern, or in combination with a number of other shapes, to create very individual border designs.

Do not feel limited to a single patterned band. Combine as many bands of different patterns as seems appropriate to the work, separating each with a narrow strip of colour. Bands of eye-jangling juxtapositions of lines, diagonals, and curves, placed side-by-side, can be effective in attracting attention.

The composition of borders is a good opportunity to emphasize certain colours within the main work. A touch of green will bring out the reds; orange will help to emphasize blues, and so on. Look at your colour wheel to find the complementary colours. These have a natural relationship, but take note that a border colour scheme that uses a completely different group of colours and tones from those of the main picture can make the border look like a totally unrelated piece of work, and this may detract from the desired effect.

A quick and effective way to try out a border idea is to glue strips of paper or fabric to different widths of heavy card. I sometimes make up three or four short strips of card, with different ideas worked on each, and lay these in the border position alongside the work. This allows me to select the best option, or it may sometimes spur a new idea.

Borders may be used to tell a completely different tale from that which is the main part of the pictorial element of the work. Alternatively, the story could continue from the centre, or main part of the work, and be carried on into the border.

BORDER MOTIFS

One way of creating a repeating pattern for a border is to take an element from the main design. If you can develop a motif taken from the main work, the border will retain a design consistency.

Cut a rectangular hole in a piece of heavy paper or card, and position this viewer over various parts of your main design to isolate an interesting area. Make several photocopies of the isolated area or trace the revealed shape. Draw a line on a separate sheet of paper and apply the repeating shapes along the line. Experiment with mirror images, with reversing or inverting motifs, or with alternate reverses and inversions. The combinations can be varied to create

The designs on a series of Little Red Riding Hood *cushions were applied by stencils. Lorna Townsend echoed her main theme in a series of border ideas. An interesting section of the design was isolated with a small square box, and all the border stencils came from this area.*

Even meaningless scrawls can be turned into creative border designs; here, Lorna has drawn some doodles on a sheet of graph paper. The squares over which the doodles passed were coloured and rearranged in several combinations to build up some interesting border designs.

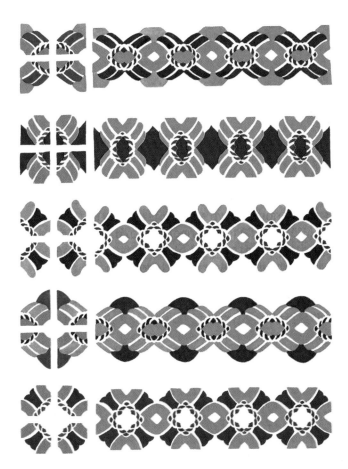

Having traced and coloured the isolated area from the main work, Lorna arranged the squares in blocks of four. Using a different corner of the box as the centre of each new design, she produced a number of interesting block designs. All the individual and unique border designs were produced in this way.

more interesting and effective patterns. Try to keep an even spacing between shapes, and make sure that they are not too distant from each other – if the spacing is over-generous, the resulting pattern may lack a feeling of continuity.

Shapes can be used as building blocks to create many interesting border designs. If you cluster four patchwork blocks in different ways, you can frequently create a range of different block patterns. Half-drop repeat patterns – brickwork style – can also be striking. Stack them row upon row until you have a pleasing effect that is suitable for framing your main design.

Any geometric shape may be developed using the same method, and border designs may be reduced or enlarged to suit the scale of the main work. In many cases it is easier to design an intricate border pattern larger than actual size, and then reduce it to suit the scale of the work.

Start with a doodle on paper. If a nice shape is created, try repeating and manipulating the shape to see how it works. You may need to alter the lines of a doodled shape, tightening and refining it so that it can be worked into a repeat pattern. Try it on graph paper. This will force the shape into neat blocks that can, again, be manipulated into pleasing designs. The graph paper will also provide a pattern for canvaswork (needlepoint) or cross stitch.

Letters of the alphabet, in various type styles, can make unique border designs. Try repeats of names, or tell the story of the fairy tale around the borders. You might use the letters in combination with bands of other designs.

SCALE AND SHAPE

Like many machines, my Pfaff computerized sewing machine is programmed with a great variety of decorative stitches and traditional geometric shapes. While these are generally quite small in scale, rows of these patterns can be built up to a good border design. The machine offers the capability of lengthening, shortening, widening or narrowing the patterns, and to begin a new colour only requires a change of the top thread.

Most people will probably recall, as children, folding up paper and cutting out repeating paper dolls. The same technique can be used to create unusual border patterns, and this is particularly easy for machine embroiderers. Lay down a strip of coloured interfacing, and place cut-outs of either sew-in or fusible interfacing over the strip. Stitch down the cut-outs and apply machine stitches to decorate the border. The interfacing will provide a sturdy medium for machine stitches.

For those with computer graphics capability, most graphics programmes have the capacity to create an immense range of repeating border effects. There will normally be libraries of simple shapes and designs of great variety. The graphics programme

ABOVE The Little Match Girl, *by Gwen Hedley, is framed on a background of dyed felt. Over the felt, dyed scrims and sheer fabrics have been applied, along with handmade paper and wrapped cords. The work combines machine embroidery with a little handstitching. The motif of the border design was developed from the flame of the candle. Size: 52 cm × 63 cm (20.5 in × 25 in).*

will painlessly size, repeat, reverse, stretch, mirror-image, invert, and otherwise manipulate motifs into countless variations. Optical scanners will allow your own tracings and drawings, plus other design sources, to be applied to your border design. The sources are unlimited, and when the border designs are completed – and it is easy to make dozens of variations – they can be printed to almost any size on a wide variety of printers, either black and white or colour.

ABOVE Gwen developed a series of border ideas incorporating motifs from the flame and trees. The shapes were cut from paper, laid down in repeating patterns, and glued to a background paper.

ABOVE Here, Lorna Townsend has worked out from the corners. There are two solutions to making a border fit the work: one is to make each of the repeat designs of a size that may be evenly divided into the measurement of each of the two (long and short) sides; where the repeat designs do not come out evenly on the work, you can create a special centrepiece to make up any differences. Insert this on any two sides of the border.

TURNING CORNERS

Corner designs for canvaswork may be developed directly on graph paper. Corner designs for stripes and other geometric shapes can be made by selecting a portion of the design and drawing a 45 degree angle across. Transfer the design to tracing paper and lay the paper across the diagonal to see the corner design. A mirror placed across the design at a 45 degree angle will also reflect the design of a mitred corner. Alternatively, a block can be designed to the width of the border, and placed in each corner, with the edges of the border strips butting against it.

As well as performing a decorative function, borders may be used in more utilitarian ways. Where quilts or coverlets are made specifically for use as bed covers, it is usually good practice to have the main design element fitted to the top surface of the bed. Borders can then be used to increase the overall size of the quilt so that it extends over the sides while retaining design integrity over the top of the bed.

When embroidered or quilted covers are used on plump cushions or pillows, designs tend to be obscured except in the very centre. This can be avoided by incorporating a toning border of the appropriate depth into the scheme.

Borders for cushions may be built up in the same way as for quilts or other embroidery. Piping, tassels, cords or a binding may be used to impart added visual interest and definition to the edges.

TRANSFERRING DESIGNS TO FABRIC

There are no definite rules for the transfer of designs to fabrics; the method must be suited to the nature of the fabric or decorative technique to be used. Some pieces of work may require very accurate transfer of design, but others may not.

If you are going to place your fabric over your cartoon and trace your design directly on the fabric; prepare the cartoon by outlining the design elements in black with a fine-tip felt pen or other suitable marker. Use permanent-ink types to avoid runny patches if it gets wet. The dark outlines will make the design more visible while tracing.

MARKING EQUIPMENT

Quilters' silver marking pencil This will not fade or smear. It can be used to draw around templates directly on the fabric.

Transfer pens and pencils Some transfer pens and pencils will leave a permanent line. If the line will show through the work, it is best to test first, to check that the pen or pencil line can be removed from the fabric.

Tailors' or dressmakers' pencils These are supplied in a variety of colours for marking on coloured fabrics. The lines may be brushed away as required.

Felt tips and fibre tips There are a number of brands of felt-tip marker designed for fabric. The line is usually blue or purple, and disappears after a period of time. The time will vary, depending upon the material and the reaction of the ink to the fabric. A variety of fibre-tip pen is also available for marking directly on the fabric. In this case, the line may be removed by moistening it with a wet brush or cotton swab (Q-tip).

PRICK AND POUNCE BY MACHINE

The prick and pounce method is used where very accurate design transfer to fine textured fabrics is required. It is not, generally, satisfactory for rough or pile fabrics.

Draw your design on tracing paper. Fix a fine needle (8-9/60-65) in the machine. Set the stitch length a little shorter than is usual for straight stitch. With no thread, and with feed dogs up and presser foot down, stitch over the design lines, making only one pass over each line. Lay the resulting pattern on the fabric and pin, tape, or baste it to the fabric.

Roll a piece of felt or other soft fabric, about 10cm (4in) wide, into a pad of about 3cm (1¼in) in diameter. Stitch it to prevent it unrolling.

Dip the end of the pad into powder. Gently rub the powder over

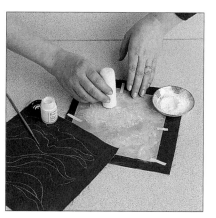

the pricked lines. Carefully lift the pattern from the fabric. Using a very fine paint brush, paint over the lines with fabric paint. Powders such as charcoal, cuttlefish bone, French chalk or talcum may be used, depending on the colour of the fabric.

TRANSFER PAINTS

These are produced in many colours. Paint the design on drawing paper. When the paint is dry, lay the paper on the fabric, painted side down. Lay a second sheet of paper over the transfer paper and press with a hot dry iron. This will produce washable and dry-cleanable colours on fabric.

TRANSFERRING TO CANVAS

Place the canvas over a tracing or drawing of the design. Using a permanent-ink, felt-tip or fabric pen, mark the design on the canvas. It is advisable to use permanent ink, so that if, for any reason, the finished piece requires washing, the ink will not dissolve and stain the work.

TEMPLATES

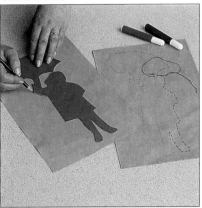

Templates can be convenient for large design areas where there is a minimum of detail. Fasten the cardboard or heavy paper template to the fabric using pins, double-sided tape, or spray glue. Trace around the outline with a fine-point, fabric paint pen (Dylon or Pebeo), or with a light pencil. Use a line of faint dots rather than heavy lines.

Appliqué templates could be composed of main elements of the tale. Pin them to the background fabric. With small stitches, baste along the edges of the template outline. When the template is removed, the exact shape will show on the background, assisting in the perfect alignment of applied pieces.

TRANSFER BY BASTING

Trace or draw the design on white tissue paper. Pin this to the fabric. Using a sharp needle and contrasting thread, baste along all the lines, taking very short stitches and an occasional back stitch to secure the thread. When all design lines are stitched, score the paper with a needle and remove it. Remove basting threads as work progresses.

PHOTOCOPY TRANSFERS

This transfers the ink (toner) to the fabric, producing a mirror image. Copies are not washable. Mix equal parts of water and white spirit (paint thinner) and one teaspoon of liquid detergent. Lay the photocopy, print side up, on a flat surface, and quickly give it a light coat of solvent, using a large watercolour brush. Position the fabric – ideally light cotton or silk – over the photocopy and apply a

second coat of solvent (do not saturate it) until it adheres to the copy. Place a few layers of fabric or paper over the transfer fabric and press with a hot iron.

WARNING Some spirits are very flammable. Do not let the iron come into direct contact with the solvent. Ensure good ventilation.

CHAPTER II

COLOURING FABRICS

For hundreds of years, the processes and arts of fabric dyeing were closely-held secrets, highly valued, guarded, and controlled by professional dyers. Fortunately, with the advent of modern chemical dyes and the ensuing mass marketing, such fabric dyeing has been simplified and made accessible to non-professionals.

Today, you do not need to be a skilled artist or an expert dyer to achieve wonderful results. For embroiderers and quilters, colouring fabric is not an end in itself, but the beginning of a process resulting in beautifully enhanced needlework.

New dyes and fabric paints for home users are usually water based and non-toxic, and most can be made permanent (fixed) through the application of heat, using a domestic iron. Many of the dyes used in industry and schools are toxic; these are quite different from the dyes available for home use and usually require special handling and processes.

The terms dye, paint, and colour, with reference to fabric colouring agents, are very ambiguous. The definition provided by the *Encyclopedia Americana* states that a 'substance can be truly termed dyed when the colour is not removed by rubbing or washing or by the action of light.' Basically, then, any agent that permanently colours a fabric is a dye. The method used to apply the dye, whether it be dipping, spraying, painting, brushing, blowing, or spattering, is irrelevant.

Since there are numerous products in the marketplace that use these terms, it is good to understand, generally, what they are and how they are used. Most manufacturers who market their dyes as 'paint' use a thick emulsion to make the painting process easier. Those products labelled as 'dye' are usually in the form of a liquid, or powder that must be made into a liquid, into which fabric is immersed.

Fabric 'colour' could be any of the above or something else.

There are dozens of manufacturers and hundreds of product names under which dyes are marketed. It is advisable before buying any product to read carefully the information on the package. This should include a description of the product and the method of use. Select a product that suits the fabric and the use to which it will be put.

Synthetic dyes have become so numerous in the marketplace that it may be difficult for the average user to discern which is best for the desired effect. For this reason, specific dyes, from which good results have been obtained, will be suggested here. If specific dyes are not available, ensure that substitute products have the characteristics required for your project.

Regardless of any particular instructions contained herein, if substitute dyes are used, always follow the manufacturer's instructions. This does not preclude any experimentation one might wish to explore.

The Goblin Market, by Christina Rossetti, provided the inspiration for Anita Faithfull in the design of her waistcoat, which has detachable sleeves. The pattern shapes in the garment are derived from medieval designs based on squares and triangles. After areas had been isolated with resist, the silk habotai fabric was painted using Pebeo Orient Express Silk paint. The waistcoat (vest) was quilted with both automatic and free machine embroidery.

PAINTING WITH RESIST ON SILK

M any fabrics may be painted, but nothing quite matches the sheen and beauty of silk. Painting on silk is a term used to describe one method of applying colour to fabric. The method may also be used to transfer designs to fabric. Colour may be applied straight to the fabric using a brush, sponge, or almost any other imaginable applicator. It is essential to separate areas of colour with a gutta resist if they are not to bleed into each other. The intentional bleeding of adjacent colours is covered later; here, we will be dealing with a dyeing process that involves the use of resist to separate colours and to create interesting designs and patterns.

PREPARING FABRICS FOR COLOURING

Silk and woollen fabrics should be gently washed in a lukewarm solution using a mild detergent specifically formulated for the fibre. This is to remove any manufacturer's dressing or natural oils that may be present in the fabric. Do not twist or wring-out these fabrics; allow them to dry naturally on towels or other absorbent material. Any wrinkles may be removed using a steam iron or with a dry iron and dampened pressing-cloth. Silk may be ironed while still wet.

Cotton, polyester-cotton blends, and all synthetic fabrics must be washed at as high a temperature as the fabric will allow. Use ordinary washing powder or liquid detergent to remove the dressing applied during the manufacturing process. Some manufacturers provide a special product to remove such dressings. It is also worth looking for fabric suppliers who specialize in the provision of fabric that has been pre-washed and is described as 'Ready to Dye'.

FABRICS FOR SILK PAINTING

Silk is available in many different weights and textures. The weight should be selected according to the technique to be used and the type of embroidery to be applied. Ensure that fabrics, threads, dyes,

interfacings, and techniques work together sympathetically before starting the main project. The heavier the fabric is, the more stitching it will support.

SILK SUBSTITUTES

Some fabric dyes, such as Deka Silk, are equally successful when used with pure cotton, polyester-silk, and synthetic fabrics. Try using gutta and dyes on remnants or other fabric scraps of the type to be used for the finished article. This will indicate the effect that the resist will have and the way in which the fabric will or will not take the dye.

FRAMES

You can use any type of frame that will allow the fabric to be firmly attached. These include artists' canvas-stretcher frames, picture frames, embroidery frames or home-made wooden frames – soft woods accept pins more readily. A coat of varnish will prevent the dye from soaking into wooden frames.

Pins that can be pushed into the wood, up to the heads, are most desirable. Use silk-pins, with their three sharp prongs, or drawing pins (thumbtacks).

ATTACHING FABRIC TO FRAMES

Cut your fabric to the exact size of the outer edge of the frame. Be sure to use a frame large enough to allow a 2.5 cm (1 in) margin around the perimeter, between the design and the frame. Pin the fabric to the frame, stretching it as taut as possible, without pulling the grain out of square.

SETTING UP A WORK AREA

Many dyestuffs are toxic, so be sure to set up your work area away from foodstuffs, and take precautions with children and animals. Replace tops on bottles as you work, to avoid accidental spillage.

Cover a clean work surface with old newspapers and/or a protective plastic cover. Many dyes are diluted with water for paler colours, so have a few small jars and clean water available.

Goblin Market, *by Anita Faithfull –
the front of the jacket is shown here.*

GUTTA

The term gutta is derived from the Southeast Asian term, gutta-percha. This clear, water-soluble substance is used to outline design areas in order to keep dye colours separated. After dyes have been applied and set, the gutta may be removed by washing in water. Some dyers choose to leave the gutta on the fabric, but it makes a white, rubbery, outline.

Alternatively, coloured or metallic-effect resists can be used and may be left in the fabric; after heat-setting, these resists will appear in a range of wonderful colours and effects.

Special gutta pipettes, with points of various sizes, are available from many dye suppliers. Nozzles of various diameters may be fitted to the pipettes and will be numbered according to size. Use the smallest available size when working on fine silks. The heavier the fabric, the larger the pipette should be, since a heavy fabric will soak up more of the resist. Gutta is placed in the pipette and applied by tracing along the lines of the cartoon or design outline.

After applying the resist, check the back of the fabric. The resist should soak through the fabric to prevent colours bleeding from one area to another. If there are any gaps, trace the lines from the back of the fabric.

DYES AND COLOURS

The dyes and paints that are suitable for silk and other fabrics are marketed under a number of brand names. I have found that Deka Silk and Pebeo Silk can easily be applied by brush and can be set with a hot iron. Another Pebeo product – Orient Express – offers a choice of steam fixing, or a rinse in their special fixing solution. A powdered product, Procion MX, may be used successfully on silk.

In any case, a wide variety of equally good dyes are to be found under other brand names, and manufacturers sometimes market the same products under different names in different countries. If you look hard enough, you will almost always find the exact shade required; if not, dyes may be mixed to achieve the correct colour. Always remember, however, that not all silk dyes are recommended for other types of fabric, and it is sensible to buy the type of dye designed for your fabric.

FIXING DYES ON FABRIC

Usually, you will want your dyes to be colour-fast to washing and dry-cleaning. Some products may be fixed (made colour-fast) by ironing. To do this, cover your ironing board with a disposable cloth to soak up excess colour. Lay an additional piece of cloth over the dyed fabric to accomplish the same purpose. Press the sandwiched fabric with a dry iron, set to the highest heat the fabric will tolerate. Steam should not be used for this process. Hold the iron on the fabric for the amount of time specified in the manufacturer's instructions. The flat-bed pressers are ideal for this.

After pressing, wash the fabric in warm water to remove excess gutta and dye. While it is still damp, press it again, between two pressing cloths, to remove wrinkles.

Manufacturers may recommend proprietary fixing products, or processes such as steam fixing. The latter will usually create more lustrous colours than fixing by ironing. However, steam fixing can be quite cumbersome to arrange, and most home dryers will find the loss of lustre through ironing less bothersome than setting up a steamer. Do not confuse the fixing requirements – some dyes requiring steam fixing can *only* be fixed by steam.

WORKING WITH PAINTED SILK

The lines left by the resist may be used as a quilting guide, and many quilts will require no further stitching than this for effective results. Machine automatic and free running stitch are easy to accomplish if the silk is stiffened with batting and a firm backing fabric. These should be securely basted together. You will not require a frame to work in this way.

Another option is to fill some of the design areas with embroidery. The silk will first need to be basted to a backing fabric, which could be as thin as organdy or organza if the piece needs to remain supple after it

has been embroidered. The silk painting technique was used for the appliqué on *Jack and the Beanstalk*.

APPLYING GUTTA

When you have established which fabrics, stitches, and colours are going to be used to express the concept of your project, silk painting can begin. Beautiful works of art can be created with this technique alone, or you might continue to embellish your design with embroidery and quilting techniques. Look at the examples of *Jack and the Beanstalk* and *Jack the Giant Killer* to see how silk painting has been used with appliqué and quilting.

Tape or otherwise secure the cartoon to a flat surface to prevent it from moving while you transfer the design. It is easiest to work from a cartoon on which the design lines have been darkened in black with a permanent-ink felt-tip pen. This will enable you to see the design through the silk, which is hampered by the fact that the frame will lift the fabric from the cartoon placed underneath. If the frame is very thick, and the gap between cartoon and fabric is so great that you cannot see the lines clearly, turn the frame over and lay the fabric side on the cartoon. Be sure to insert a small spacer at each corner to lift the fabric from the cartoon. This prevents the fabric from adhering to the cartoon and also avoids the possible transfer of inks from cartoon to fabric, through the solvent action of the gutta. If the fabric is so dense that you cannot see the cartoon, place a light source behind the cartoon.

When painting over large design areas, load as large a brush as is practical and quickly lay down the colour. To avoid the appearance of join-lines (like watermarks), try to lay all the colour in each area before it has time to dry. Do not attempt to paint accurately into tight corners, close to the gutta. The capillary action of the fabric will draw the paint into tight areas. Any paint that you apply over the gutta line will colour the adjacent area.

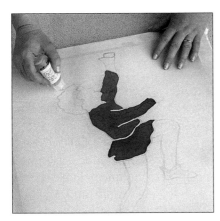

1 Trace the outline of the cartoon to a piece of stiff cardboard, using an indelible pen or marker. Insert the card under the frame, close to the silk, so that the tracing may be seen through the fabric. Keep a space between the cardboard and the silk or the resist may adhere to it. Trace the design outlines, using gutta.

2 After the gutta has thoroughly dried, paint the isolated areas in the chosen colours, using a watercolour brush.

BELOW *Denise Harrison was once again inspired by* Tales of Mabinogion *in her framed panel* Branwen Returning, *which depicts Branwen and the seven surviving Welshmen returning to Anglesey after the war in Ireland. After applying resist, she painted and then quilted the silk panel. The borders are mainly decorated with free machine embroidery, with thicker threads couched by machine and by hand.*

THE SERENDIPITY OF MISTAKES

I have yet to find the person who can work without mistakes. The trick is to turn a mistake into a wonderful, unplanned creation. Try wetting the area on which the unplanned error has occurred; over this, sprinkle some salt (table or rock salt). Each type of salt will create a different effect. Add a bit more colour, if you choose, to make the error look deliberate. Remember that for needleworkers the painting and dyeing is only a starting point for other work – stitches and other fabric manipulation will alter and improve your design.

Loading the fabric with several layers of fabric paint will cause a significant reduction in the sheen of the fabric, however. Iron-fixed dyes used full strength, or only slightly diluted, will also reduce the sheen.

COLOUR SAMPLERS

Before beginning a project it is a good idea, as already explained, to take some time to experiment with fabric, dyes, and gutta. This will indicate how the materials will work together and how they may be used to express the concept.

Always keep a notebook handy and make as accurate a record as possible of the exact proportions and mixes used; there is nothing more infuriating than the perfect, but unrepeatable, recipe.

It may be helpful to dye swatches of every colour in the range to keep as a visual record for this project and others. With each dye batch, keep personal notes about the success or failure of the dyeing session.

COLOUR MIXING

Mix a wide range of the colours you would like to use in your project. Dyes, as supplied by the manufacturers, can be very intense. Some may require dilution ranging from one to ten parts water or alcohol (methylated spirits). Observe the spread of dye on the fabric and the resultant colour and intensity. If you dilute the dye, this will of course lighten the colour. Using standard colour theory, primary colours – red, blue and yellow – may be mixed to create other colours. Most manufacturers supply a full spectrum of shades of every colour, and most people will find this range sufficient.

ABOVE *It is possible to get two prints from the fabric paint applied to the glass.*

LEFT *The frame has been set up for dyeing a colour sampler. Undiluted dyes are in the small glass containers; larger glass jars contain dyes diluted with water. The circular shapes were outlined with resist and a wide range of one manufacturer's supplies have been applied without mixing colours.*

ABOVE *A marbled effect can be created by applying dye directly to fabric with an ordinary household paintbrush. The technique works best on silk; the dye does not spread as easily on other fabrics.*

ABOVE *Samples of dyed fabrics*
1 *Fairy tale trees painted with Dylon Glossy Paint.*
2 *Examples of Deka resist colours – the resist may be left in the fabric if desired.*
3 *Many colours were painted on silk fabric using silk dyes.*
4 *A wash was applied to the orange fabric. Designs were drawn using Dylon Glossy Paint, Glitter Paint, Puff Paint, and metallic powders.*
5 *This sample was dyed and stitched by Vivien Prideaux.*
6 *Dragon painted on silk using resist by Jan Stubbenhagen.*

LAYING A WASH ON BACKGROUND FABRIC

For some people, just picking up a fabric, feeling it, and looking at it will provide spontaneous inspiration. This added stimulus is helpful if you are not particularly happy with your cartoon. Other people will feel the creative urge develop as they apply dyes and paints to the fabric. If you have developed a wonderful cartoon with lots of colour and texture, it may be disappointingly difficult to convert it to fabric, but remember that all of these techniques are starting points. Do not slavishly try to translate from one medium to another; be experimental, and let the effects of dyes, paints, and colour direct you into the evolution of a truly creative work. Remain open to new images as you work from stage to stage.

Like the painter facing a stark white canvas, the embroiderer can be intimidated by the prospect of a blank white fabric. A wash of colour can be a good starting point on any fabric. Nothing in nature is ever one solid colour. Try laying a wash of several colours, or a wash of many shades of a single colour. Use one or more dyeing or painting techniques. If you find the idea of drawing intimidating, a background wash can often be a good inspirational starting point for stitches.

I use a wash to create a background for appliqué, as have others whose technique is shown throughout the book. *Jack and the Beanstalk, Jack the Giant Killer,* and *The Princess and the Pea* are all examples of this.

WASH ON SILK AND OTHER FABRICS

The dyes and colours used for painting on silk (see pages 30–1) may be used for this technique. A background wash may be applied to good effect not only on silk, but on numerous other fabrics as well. Try using a variety of fabrics in a single piece of work – the wash can be applied on any weight of cotton, from very light to heavy duck, though heavy fabrics will take longer to dry. Polyester-cottons, silk substitutes and velvets will respond to a wash. Deka Silk or Pebeo Silk may be used in full strength or diluted. Pebeo's

Seta Colour, Dylon's Color Fun, or any of the fabric paints that can be fixed by iron are also acceptable. Most fabric paints will require some dilution to make them thin enough to apply as a wash.

APPLYING WASH

Frame your fabric as is explained on page 30. Use a household paint brush 5–7.5 cm (2–3 in) wide, or some other suitable applicator – brushes made of sponge are available at art supply shops and are ideal for this purpose. Merging-colour effects may be created by applying more than one colour to the fabric. The colours will spread more quickly if the fabric is sprayed with water before you apply the paint, and rivulets of colour will form if the frame is tilted while the fabric is still wet. The fabric may be left to dry naturally, or you can dry it more quickly with a hair dryer.

PAINTING OR DRAWING OVER WASH

After the paint has dried and been fixed, other colours may be painted over the wash. Try wetting the fabric and laying on different colours. The thicker fabric paints may be applied over stencils or templates, using sponges, rollers or corks.

Fabric pens, such as Pebeo Seta Skrib or Dylon Color Fun Markers, can be used to draw freehand designs over or under the wash. Permanent pens are available in many colours and may also be used.

MARBLING FABRIC

This technique creates a marbled effect on fabric. As with all fabric dyeing, you must first ensure that the fabric is prepared for dyeing. Organize the work area as for painting on silk. Soak the fabric in clear water until it has been thoroughly wetted, then wring out excess water and lay it over plastic sheeting.

Deka Silk dyes may be used for this process, though fabrics of blended fibres will dye unevenly. Most dye colours, when prepared according to the manufacturer's instructions, are very intense. Softer

The Lion and the Gnat, *by Penny Butterworth, is a framed panel inspired by the ancient Greek fabulist, Aesop. Three-dimensional pieces were applied by machine to a marbled background. Around the bottom of the picture is a line from the fable: 'The least of our enemies is often the most to be feared.' Size: 58 cm (23 in) square.*

shades may be had by diluting the dye, adding water until the desired colour is achieved. The dyes will, in any case, spread more easily when they are diluted.

Using a paint brush 5–10 cm (2–4 in) wide, apply the dye to the fabric. Several colours may be applied. Silk, in particular, tends to dry quickly, and dry fabric inhibits the spread of the dye, so if the fabric begins to dry, spray it with water.

After you have applied the dye, the marbling is achieved by sprinkling salt over the fabric while it is still wet. You can achieve different mottling effects with coarse and fine granules. Let the fabric dry naturally; this process could take from one to three days, depending upon the weight of the fabric.

VARIATIONS

Interesting variations may be achieved by using a patterned or textured plastic sheet. You might try hot salt sprinkled over the dyed fabric, or crush and squeeze, or severely twist the fabric. Drops of undi-luted dye may be dripped over the wet, dyed, fabric for other unusual effects.

Another idea is to paint dry fabric, allowing the brush marks to form a part of the design. A sponge would create a different effect, or you could use a medicine dropper to form droplets of colour. Any of these methods might help you to cover the fabric with bold and imaginative fairy tale colours, without too much concern for intricate design.

PRINTING FROM GLASS

Random patterns of colour may be achieved through the use of thick panes of window glass. Drop spoon-fuls of fabric paint on a pane of glass. Stir through the different colours until they are slightly mixed. Lay a second pane of glass over the top of the first. The paint will radiate out in random patterns under the pressure of the glass. Lift off the top piece of glass. The paint will create some surface tension between the glass panes. (If the top pane has been laid slightly askew it will be easier to get a grip to separate the two.) You will now have two dye transfers. Carefully lay very fine cotton or silk over one of the panes. Pat the fabric gently to assist the transfer of paint. Care-fully lift the dyed fabric from the glass and allow it to dry naturally on a flat surface. Other shiny and paint-repellant surfaces will create similar effects.

A RANGE OF FABRIC SHADES

I f you wish to use many shades of a single colour, it may be difficult to find a fabric shop that stocks the necessary range. As a result, you may have to dye fabrics for yourself.

A wide variety of hot- and warm-water dyes is available, some of which may be used in your domestic washing machine. The washing machine method demands that materials be dyed one shade at a time. To achieve a range of shades, therefore, you must use a diminishing quantity of dye powder of the same colour in each batch. For example, use a full packet of dye for the first batch, ¾ of a packet for the next, and so on. Machine-dyeing should produce even colouring, without watermarks or crease lines in the fabric.

Soft water will assist in achieving a good even colour. Always use the correct measure of any additive listed on the instructions for any dye; dyeing is very much a chemical process, and as such may demand certain additives or temperatures to create the correct action.

I have had particular success with Deka Textile Dye Series L for monochromatic fabric dyeing. This dye, however, requires controlled heat during the dyeing process. A unit used by mothers to boil nappies (diapers) is very useful; it holds about 14–18 l (3–4 gal) of water and is thermostatically controlled. If you have a large enough container you can dye fabric on your stove. A dyeing thermometer might be useful but it is not essential – most dyebaths only require that the temperature remains just under boiling. Whatever vessel you use, it must be large enough for the fabric to swim freely in the dyebath.

Hanks of thread, silks, wools, and cottons may be dyed using the same process: place a dowel, or wooden spoon over the top of the vessel; tie a thread to each hank, and fasten it to the dowel, leaving a sufficient length for the dyeing threads to swim freely in the dyebath. Each hank may then be extracted from the dyebath from time to time to check the colour.

CAUTION Do not dye in vessels which are also used for cooking.
Wear a protective mask when using any dye powders.

The following are recipes for specific dye products, but there are many other dyes available. Be sure to follow manufacturer's instructions for substitutes.

DEKA TEXTILE DYE – SERIES L
This formula is for cotton, linen, jute and other plant fibres, to achieve a consistent, even colour.
The given quantity will dye 240 g (8 oz) of fabric.

1 tablespoon dye powder (1 packet = 10 g/1 tablespoon)
2 tablespoons salt
4.5–5.75 l (4–5 British qt/5–6 US qt) boiling water

Boil 3.5 l (3 [3¾] qt) of water in the dyeing vessel. In a separate container, dissolve salt and dye in 1 litre (1 [1] qt) boiling water. Add the dissolved dye/salt to the water in the dyeing vessel. Maintain the temperature of the dyebath at 80–90°C (175–195°F), just below boiling. Add thoroughly wetted, prepared (see pages 26–7) fabric to the dyebath.

Add additional hot water to the dyebath, if necessary, to ensure that the fabric swims freely.

For maximum colour intensity, leave the fabric in the dyebath for 15 to 30 minutes while stirring constantly. Shorter durations may give a less intense colour, resulting in pale pastels. Continued use of the same dyebath will result in a reduction of colour intensity.

Shades of one colour Start with a dyebath of the most intense colour. Continually check the fabric for desired colour intensity. Remove the fabric from the dyebath when the correct colour is achieved. Add more water and more fabric to the dyebath, until a good colour is achieved, remembering to raise the temperature to 80–90°C (175–195°F).

Again, continually check the fabric for the desired colour intensity and remove it when it has reached the correct shade. Continue this procedure to achieve decreasing colour intensities. Dyes will deplete rapidly, and experience indicates that a maximum number of three batches is feasible.

After dyeing is completed, rinse the fabric under cold running water until the water runs clear. When dyeing is accomplished at the recommended temperature, no fixative is required. Finally, wash the fabric in hot soapy water and dry it before using. If you cannot dye at the recommended temperature, there is a proprietary fixative for this dye.

The intensity of the final colour depends upon the concentration of the dyebath, the amount of time the fabric stays in the bath, and the quantity of fabric dyed.

Formula for silks and woollens
The quantity will dye 240g (8oz) fabric or thread.

> 1 tablespoon dye powder (1 packet = 10g/1 tablespoon)
> 1l (1 [1] qt) boiling water
> 3.5–4.5l (3–4 [3¾–4] qt) warm water
> 75ml (3fl oz) or 5 tablespoons distilled vinegar

Dissolve the dye and vinegar in boiling water. Add the warm water to the dye solution. Adjust the dyebath to a temperature of 50°C (125°F). Add thoroughly wetted fabric to the dyebath.

Add additional warm water to the dyebath, if necessary, to ensure that the fabric swims freely.

Slowly raise the dyebath temperature to the highest temperature that the fabric will tolerate, keeping it below boiling. Maintain the temperature, while constantly stirring the fabric, for 30 minutes.

Allow the water to cool with the fabric in the dyebath. When it is cool, rinse the fabric in cool running water until the water runs clear. Hang the dripping fabric to air dry.

SHADING AND MOTTLING EFFECTS

Warm- and cold-water dyes may be used for shading and mottling effects. The Deka L Dye series may be used in lower temperature dyebaths. Because of the lower temperatures, plastic or other containers may be used. Procion MX or Dylon dyes may be used in a similar way – refer to the individual manufacturer's instructions.

Mottled effects are created by not stirring the fabric in the dyebath, or by stirring infrequently, and by dipping fabrics into more than one colour while they are still wet. Fabrics may be over-dyed several times for multiple colours.

When air drying fabrics, do not fold them over a clothes line. This will leave fade marks on the fabric.

Bluebeard – *a page from a book by Gillian Swift, using applied dyed fabrics and machine embroidery.*

STENCILS

S tencilling is another artistic technique that has been used worldwide for centuries. In the United States, during the 19th century, ready-made printed fabrics and other decorated products were hard to come by. Those products that were available usually came from Europe and were very expensive to purchase.

The amount of stencilling used for any work is a matter of personal choice. The cartoons used for stencil design should be very simple outline shapes. A full-colour cartoon will indicate the number of stencils needed for the design, each colour requiring a separate stencil. If you are new to stencilling, try limiting your colours to two or three. As confidence builds, use more colours and more complex shapes.

Stencilling may be applied over white or off-white as well as dyed fabrics. The resulting colour will be affected by the background colour. To dye the background after stencilling, save the inside cut-out of the stencil shape (template), or cut another piece of the exact shape. Lay this template over the stencilled area to screen it while you apply the background colour. If you are using this method it is best to apply the background colour with a spray. Both stencils and templates were used freely to apply shapes to the *Jack and the Beanstalk* background.

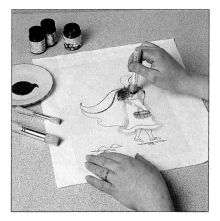

1 For *Little Red Riding Hood*, Lorna Townsend photocopied her entire cartoon to five acetate transparencies. The cartoon was separated into five colours, and a transparency made for each colour. All the layers were stacked together to ensure that the shapes registered with each other. A stencil was made for each colour by cutting the shapes of that colour from each transparency. To avoid confusion, the name of the associated colour was written on each transparency.

2 Align the stencil on the fabric in the correct position. Using a dabbing motion with a stencil brush or sponge, apply fabric paint, progressing from light to dark colours. Let each colour dry before laying down another stencil. Shapes may be shaded by adding colour over the same cut-out (again wait until the first application is dry).

3 The shape cut from a stencil is called a template, and may also be used as a design element. Hold the template firmly to the fabric with your fingers. Daub around the edges with paints – this will result in a design that looks more free. Either the template or the stencil may be moved around the fabric to build up a design incorporating different colours and orientations of the same shape. Here, background leaf and tree shapes have been built up by moving templates and stencils freely around the fabric.

Lorna Townsend stencilled the shapes for these cushions on silk and cotton fabrics and then airbrushed the background. The author used free machine embroidery over the stencilled lines.

The stencilled fabric could be used on its own or embellished with any of several embroidery techniques.

PAINTS

Deka Permanent, Elbetex, Dylon Color Fun and Pebeo Seta Colour are all suitable, but other pastes or paints with a thick consistency may be used. Most of these are available in fairy-like, iridescent colours. Ensure that any fabric paints used are iron-fixable.

STENCILS

Purpose-made stencil paper is the obvious choice for stencils, but stencils may also be cut from heavy oiled or waxed paper, or from acetate film (contact paper). Alternatively, you can use heavy cardboard or stiff paper, but stencils of this type must be sprayed with automobile spray enamels, or other sealer, to stop them soaking up the fabric paints. Most stencils may be held on the fabric by hand. However, if the shapes are very complex or require accurate alignment, it is best to secure them into position on the fabric, with masking tape.

When cutting stencils, protect the work surface with a cutting mat, stiff card, or a piece of heavy glass. Use a stencil cutter, scalpel, or sharp-pointed craft knife to cut the shapes.

FABRICS

To maintain paint within the stencil shape, use silk or cotton that is medium to heavy in weight and has been washed and ironed. Fabric paint has a tendency to spread under the edges of the stencil when used on very thin fabrics.

PREPARATIONS

Pin the fabric to be stencilled to a cork, polystyrene, or fabric-covered board to hold it firmly in position for stencilling. Pour paints into a flat container, such as a saucer, into which you can easily dip stencil brushes or sponges. Keep a separate sponge for each colour. If you can afford to set aside a stencil brush for each colour you will also save a lot of rinsing out between colour applications.

CHAPTER III

APPLIQUE

Both the ancient Egyptians and the Greeks used appliqué in their textiles.
Styles change over the years, but the basic techniques remain the same.
Essentially, appliqué entails laying a fabric shape against a background and
stitching around the shape to apply the fabric to the background.

A nything that may be laid on a fabric and stitched down comes under the heading of appliqué, including buttons, bows and beads, as well as fabrics of all kinds.

Large pieces of work, such as quilts, wall hangings, pillow covers and garments, may incorporate this technique. Appliqué designs can often be accomplished much more quickly than those using other needlework techniques. Many types of appliqué – especially those types that are worked by machine – can be very hard wearing, and lend themselves to decorating children's clothing.

A number of appliqué techniques are explored in the succeeding pages, including whole piece appliqué, appliqué with cut-out shapes, manipulated appliqué, and appliqué both by hand and by machine. The technique lends itself to design by paper collage, and if you are going to pursue your own design concepts in appliqué, you should also refer to the section on cartoons on pages 14–15.

The advent of the domestic sewing machine opened new vistas to needleworkers. The use of machine appliqué produces results that are as varied as the people who choose this technique. A domestic sewing machine may be used to attach the applied fabric through the use of standard zigzag, satin, or other decorative stitches.

Numerous colours and layers may be combined to create a glorious range of colour and contour, which is one reason why appliqué is a favourite choice for designs representing figures of people and animals.

RIGHT Princess Marigold *is a fairy tale written by Gillian Pugh for her two sons. The castle and background hills are worked in shadow appliqué. The quilt was assembled in sections and joined by machine stitching. The patchwork border and binding were added after the quilt was completed. Size: 137cm × 163cm (54in × 64in).*

ABOVE *The tree looming on the left has two pockets. One of these is the hiding place of a witch, who is secured to the quilt by a ribbon stitched to the tree. The other pocket is the repository of a tiny book in which the tale is recorded.*

PLANNING LARGE PIECES

Planning a large piece of work, such as a quilt, can be a daunting task. I have found a number of ways to approach the planning and design of larger pieces, and some tips are also offered by contributors whose work appears in this chapter. One of the first considerations should be to determine the size of the quilt. Another is that the selection of the techniques and fabrics should reflect the use to which the quilt will be put. Some quilts will be functional, being used on a day-to-day basis as a bed cover. Others may be destined to be wall hangings, in which case the wear-and-tear will be minimal. Functional items will probably dictate washable fabrics and dyes, as well as fairly sturdy threads and secure decorative stitching techniques. Budgetary factors may also limit the choice of fabrics, threads, and other materials.

Paper for creating full-sized quilt designs can be found in fairly large widths. When in difficulties, I have used wide widths of sew-in interfacing. The interfacing is convenient to fold up and store, and does not deteriorate too much.

It is very convenient to allocate a special drawer in which to store all of the design papers, fabrics, threads, notebooks, books, and other inspirational materials for each project, and you should ideally include drawing paper and media. This organization makes it very easy to pick up the project quickly and work on it as short periods of time permit. Keep some pictures and drawings pinned up in your work area. This will spur you to more thoughts and keep the project alive, even when you are not actively working upon it. Test some of the techniques you may have in mind before committing yourself to the whole quilt.

EXTRACTS FROM A QUILTER'S NOTEBOOK

One of the best ways of organizing your quilting activities is to keep a notebook to record ideas and developments on projects. Keep a record of ideas as they develop, and do not trust to memory from week to week. Log your time as you work on a project, including research in libraries or scanning magazines and other sources for your project. All that creative thinking counts. Carry the notebook with you at all times; you can never tell when some inspirational idea will come, nor from what source. The following are some entries from a typical notebook.

June 1 Decided to tackle a quilt for Anthony (8 years old). He is a keen sci-fi fan. He would like a quilt to hang on his wall, facing the door, so all his friends will see it as they walk into his room. Will still need to be fairly practical... may use it on his bed sometimes. Should be washable. Size: decided to make it to fit his bed.

June 18 Anthony has given me some posters and books with all the characters he wants featured on the quilt. Watching a sci-fi video tonight. Maybe more ideas will come.

Evening Wonderful colours and characters. We have narrowed down to two characters, a robot and

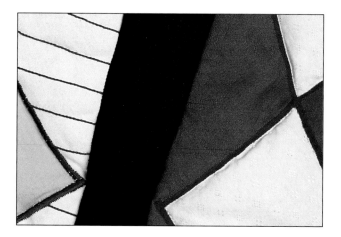

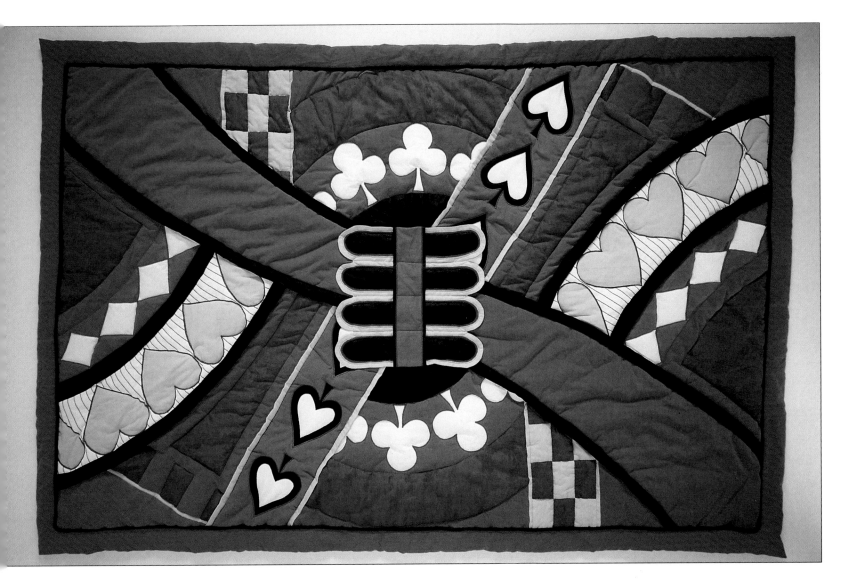

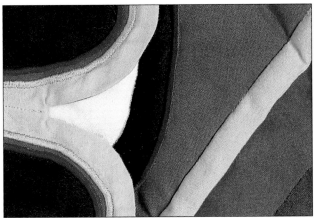

ABOVE *To make the* Playing Card *quilt for her son, Angela Howard first dyed her fabrics in the range of colours that she had selected to use on the project. She incorporated both appliqué and cut-back appliqué into the design, and machine quilted over the top. Size: 183 cm × 122 cm (72 in × 48 in).*

FAR LEFT *The blue stitchery is a hand embroidery thread applied by machine cable stitch. For this technique, the needle carries an ordinary sewing thread; the special thread is wound on the bobbin, and the fabric is turned face down during stitching.*

LEFT *Automatic satin stitch was used to embellish the design and fill in areas that had been cut back.*

an alien hero. Think I will try to position them in front of spaceship.

June 19 Decided to concentrate on developing cartoon before worrying about fabric and threads. Will need to use appliqué as the main technique. Will paint people, atmosphere and backgrounds. Would like to do the quilting by machine.

June 24 Made a collage of some effects from sci-fi videos. Proportioned design to shape of finished piece. Traced some basic shapes... making up costumes, etc., to draw on. We've done 3 tracings. A. is colouring one.

June 26 Divided one of the tracings into grids to enlarge on photocopier.

Evening Laid quilt-sized paper on the floor... put enlarged grids down. Looks like giant jigsaw puzzle. Hung design on the wall. Characters need more detail after blowing up to size. Will fill in background of cartoon with poster paint, big felt-tips, and crayons.

June 28 Fabric shopping today. Shop gave me fabric swatches to try to match colours. Hard to find the exact colours I want to use. Decided I will paint and dye fabrics in colours I can't find.

PLANNING FOR MACHINE STITCHING

Large pieces can be very cumbersome to put through the sewing machine. This is especially true if you are turning many corners and attempting to use the needle as a pencil for free machine embroidery. This problem may be overcome if the quilt is planned in manageable sections to be joined later.

Where a large amount of appliqué or machine embroidery is planned, the pieces must be of such a size as to allow manipulation under the machine, even when bearing in mind that sections may be rolled to fit under the machine and unrolled as stitching progresses.

DESIGNING A QUILT

Angela Howard wanted to make a quilt for her son based upon the Lewis Carroll story *Alice in Wonderland*. After considering all the related allusions in the story, she decided to take her inspiration from a deck of playing cards. She liked the bright bold colours and simplistic designs, and felt they would lend themselves to her idea.

To isolate some interesting, eye-pleasing design sections, she cut a viewing hole in a piece of paper and placed it over areas of the playing cards. These she enlarged on a photocopier, made mirror images, and changed lines and patterns to create an aesthetically pleasing design. With an eye to a possible patchwork design, Angela cut a series of stencil shapes from some of her first efforts. The patchwork idea was then rejected in favour of appliqué.

The next task was to seek out a variety of white fabrics, some plain and others with texture. Since the quilt was going to be produced in bright primary colours, combined with white and black, the textures might soften the effect. After many experiments, she elected to use cotton sheeting, cotton damask, polycotton sheeting, and cotton sateen. A further factor in favour of these fabrics was their washability; this was to be a functional bed quilt, not just a hanging, and it therefore needed to be washable.

Thread selection was also an important consideration. For strong quilting, she chose dressmakers' threads, but for satin stitch, she decided to use lustrous machine embroidery threads. The end-use of the quilt seemed to dictate a 100g (4oz) batting; with hindsight, Angela now believes that a lighter batting would have been much easier to machine.

Experiments with many techniques led her to a combination of cut-back appliqué and automatic machine quilting. The top was worked in several pieces and put together in jigsaw-puzzle-fashion, with interlocking and overlapping pieces. The lining was cut larger than the front fabric. It was lock-stitched to the back of the quilt, the excess fabric being brought to the front to act as a border with mitred corners.

ABOVE *Here are a couple of Angela's many design exercises. The surest pathway to a successful design is to experiment with as many ideas as possible.*

RIGHT *It is important to balance colour proportions correctly, and one way to do this is to make colour bars. These reduce the colours to be used, and their quantity in relation to each other, to a bar graph. Pencils or felt-tips can be used to make a chart, or you can wind threads of the appropriate colours around a thin strip of cardboard, in bands of varying thickness. Angela made a series of colour bars to help her to visualize the colours before she shopped for fabrics.*

The colours indicated on colour charts and dye packets can be deceptive. Angela tested all of her dyes on the fabrics that she had chosen, to ensure that she could reproduce the desired colours.

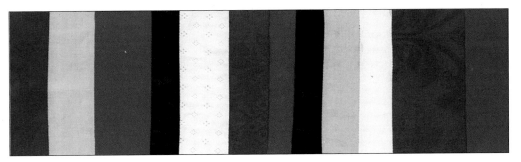

A MACHINE APPLIQUED QUILT

There are a few techniques and hints that will help you to achieve satisfactory results with appliqué. I have found it advisable to avoid applying figures and shapes smaller than about 5 cm (2 in) either way. Tiny shapes can be very difficult to stitch, especially if there are sharp bends and corners, so it is best to avoid very small details, such as fingers and small profiles of faces. Try to simplify shapes wherever possible.

Larger shapes – 30–45 cm (12–18 in) across – have a tendency to stretch and sag. The larger shapes may be controlled by stitching through the appliqué at various places before applying zigzag or machine satin stitch around the edges. Most figures will be made up of composite parts, such as arms or legs; to keep the size of pieces manageable, each of these may be applied separately.

There are various considerations to bear in mind when selecting the type of appliqué to use. If shapes are very intricate and have angular juxtapositions, the whole-piece method (see pages 48–9) should be considered. This method is quite a good way for beginners to hone their technique. Cut-out shapes are effective where fairly straightforward simple patterns are used. Cut-back appliqué is a slightly more advanced technique, and could be useful to those with some experience in appliqué techniques.

With all forms of appliqué, it is important to ensure that the selvedges of the background fabric and the applied fabrics run in the same direction. This is generally referred to as aligning the grain of the fabrics. This, and other preparations for appliqué, are important to successful work. Whichever technique you are using, baste the appliqué shape to the background fabric before doing any edge stitching. Always baste from the centre of the shape, radiating outward to the edges.

When working from your cartoon, it may be necessary to transfer the design to the background fabric in order to position the applied pieces accurately. Refer to the section on design transfer.

Robert Burns' famous dictum that the best-laid schemes of mice and men often go awry is certainly true of appliqué – even the best-planned work can go wrong. One of the most common problems is puckering, though this can normally be prevented by thorough basting. If you find that either your background or the applied fabric is beginning to pucker, turn to the back of the work. With sharp scissors, remove some of the background fabric from behind the applied fabric, pressing the fabric out as you cut. Do not try to cut too near the stitching; leave a fabric allowance of about 1.5 cm (⅝ in) around any stitching. Cut away as many pieces of background fabric as may be needed to correct the situation. If you have to carry out any corrective work of this type you will require a lining over the back.

APPLIQUE FABRICS

Background fabric The background fabric should be heavier than the applied fabric. You can use virtually any fabric, from silk, to velvet, or washable furnishing fabric. If you wish to incorporate trapunto in the work to create a sculptural effect, baste a lining fabric to the wrong side of the background fabric. Do this before applying any shapes. Cotton muslin or sheeting may be used for the lining.

Applied fabric The top fabric, or the fabric to be applied, should be of a similar weight to or lighter than the background. Avoid fabrics that are stretchy or fray easily unless this is the effect sought. Almost any kind of fabric may be used for appliqué, ranging from light or transparent materials, such as nylon,

*To make Jack and the Beanstalk, Jack's body was first outlined in resist and painted on silk. A heavier silk fabric was chosen for the background, and stencils were used for leaves and bean pods. Jack's figure was applied to the background fabric with automatic zigzag stitch.
The author then quilted over the entire piece with free machine stitching. Size: 69 cm × 51 cm (27 in × 20 in).*

organdy and nets, to leather, felt and plastics. Many of these fabrics or materials may be layered before being applied. Hot-water-soluble fabric and vanishing muslin may be used to create machine lace.

INTERFACING FOR APPLIED FABRICS

An interfacing will give body to very thin or stretchy fabrics and will prevent fraying. Different types will produce a variety of effects. Interfacings can considerably alter the stiffness of the fabric, so it is best to avoid using interfacing on very large pieces.

Paper interfacings Known as Stitch-and-Tear, or by other trade names, this is the key to successful machine satin stitch, and can be used to strengthen fabric when it is being subjected to any kind of heavy, automatic machine stitching. Place the Stitch-and-Tear under the fabric. When stitching is complete, turn the fabric over and gently tear away the paper.

Bonding paper (transfer fusing web) This is an adhesive that is bonded to paper. It is useful in bonding appliqué shapes to background fabrics. Try bonding to transparent fabrics, or to dissolving fabrics. As always, be sure to read the manufacturer's instructions.

The transfer of the adhesive to the background fabric will cause a slight stiffening. Machine embroiderers prefer to work on a slightly stiff fabric, but quilters may find the fabric will not fall into the soft undulating hills and valleys of their creations.

BATTING

Batting is available in a range of materials extending from silk to cotton and synthetics. Some suppliers may have a compressed fabric that can be used as a batting substitute. Lightweight (56g/2oz) batting is effective for quilted appliqué. It is difficult to machine intricate details through thicker batting.

LINING

The lining for an appliqué quilt may be a single layer of fabric, of a similar weight to the front fabric. Some artists also decorate the back of their work, making it reversible.

WHOLE-PIECE APPLIQUE

This method has been called 'whole-piece' appliqué, because the applied fabric is larger than the finished shape will be, and it is not necessary to cut out each shape before applying it to the background. I normally do a considerable amount of work on the fabric before it is applied, and this helps to overcome the problem of buckling as stitching is worked.

First, frame the fabric in order to apply watered-down fabric paint or use silk painting techniques (see pages 30–31). This is done *before* the fabric is applied. In this case, the thinned fabric paints will not require the application of gutta, since the colours will not spread very much on thicker fabrics. Even if the paint runs outside the outline of the shape to be applied, do not be too concerned. Fabric outside the design outline will be cut away. The fabric may be applied after it has been painted, and free machine embroidery may be added to the design, but put the fabric in an embroidery ring first.

When machine stitching with zigzag or satin stitch around the edges, do not let the frame confuse you. Allow the machine to feed the fabric through as normal, and do not try to push the fabric through the feed dogs of the machine. The frame will make it much easier to turn corners or angles. The frame also aids in the production of an even satin stitch. If Stitch-and-Tear is used with the fabric, it will not need to be basted. Place the Stitch-and-Tear under the fabric. Be sure to remove the Stitch-and-Tear after completing stitches. This method allows you to apply complex shapes with relative ease.

Silk can be a very expensive fabric to use. I try to conserve the silk as much as possible, but when the fabrics need to be framed, there can be a large amount of waste. To extend the working area, I usually stitch a border of cotton fabric around the edges, as near to the design outline as possible.

In the example, a wash has been applied to the background fabric. The piece to be applied, Jack's figure, has also been painted. Both the background and the applied piece had been carefully planned to fit together. This piece could be used as a finished work without the addition of any stitches or it may be developed as indicated.

1 Cut a paper template of the chosen shape – in this case Jack's figure – tracing it from the main cartoon. Pin the template in the correct position to the background fabric. Using dark thread, baste around the shape, forming an outline. Remove the template.

2 Align the fabric with the painted figure over the dark threads. If necessary, hold the two fabrics up to a window to align the figure. Securely pin the two fabrics together.

3 Carefully baste the fabric to be appliquéd in position on the background fabric. Thorough basting is important in securing large pieces so they do not pucker and buckle when stitching is applied. Beginning in the centre, stitch toward the outer edge, with lines of basting radiating around the piece. Add a line of basting around the perimeter of the piece.

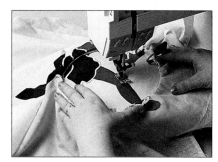

4 Set your machine for straight stitch and stitch around the shape of your appliqué figure. Carefully follow the line of the figure.

The excess applied fabric is now ready to be trimmed away. Using very sharp small scissors, carefully cut away the excess fabric, trimming it as near to the stitching as possible.

5 Mount the work in a large embroidery frame. The frame will need to be repositioned as work progresses. Alternatively, if the fabric is supported with Stitch-and-Tear, no embroidery frame is required. Apply zigzag or satin stitch around the cut edges of the shapes.

LEFT *Decorative and utility stitch patterns, of the type used to embellish the bottom of Jack's tunic, are available on most automatic and computerized machines.*

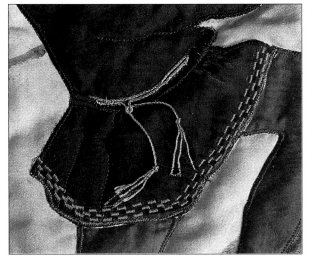

APPLIQUE WITH CUT-OUT SHAPES

Much machine appliqué is accomplished through the use of cut-out shapes. Any stitching, painting, manipulation, or other decoration of the cut-out pieces should be done before they are cut to shape.

Small flat shapes can be held in position on the background fabric by applying a small amount of aerosol spray glue to the back of the shape. Larger pieces should be thoroughly basted to secure them for stitching. When the pieces are positioned, work straight or free machine stitches around the edges. This stitching may be left as it is, or additional decorative stitches can be worked. The appliquéd fabric

can then be decorated with other techniques such as quilting.

Alternatively, shapes can be padded by placing felt, perhaps in several layers, or batting in the correct position on the background fabric. These underlying layers can be attached with either stitches or a spray of glue. The final appliquéd shape will have to be cut slightly larger to accommodate the added thickness of the padding.

Before deciding upon the fabric to be used for the appliqué, it is important to determine whether the piece will require washing or dry-cleaning. Certain items, including some wall hangings, panels, and fairy tale books, will probably require washing.

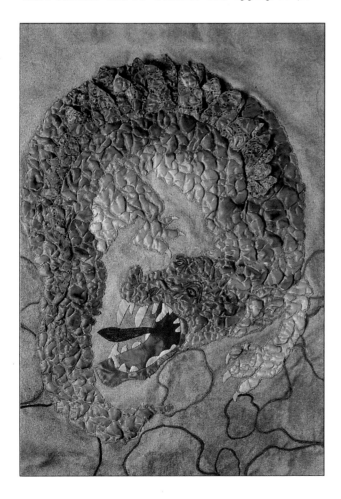

LEFT *Fay Twydell selected a heavy cotton duck for the background of* Saint George and the Dragon. *Over this she sprayed automobile enamels. The nylon organza of the dragon was heat seared to create a bubbly, scaly effect. Free machine embroidery contributes additional textural effects, and was also used to apply the dragon to the background. Size: 107 cm × 84 cm (42 in × 33 in).*

ABOVE *The Tournament is a medieval-style triptych by Adrianne Woodfine. When open, the triptych depicts a tournament in progress. The blue and bronze background squares were created in cut-back appliqué. Adrianne's sister has now written a fairy tale based on the work. Size: 64 cm × 38 cm (25 in × 15 in) unfolded.*

Most machine manufacturers supply a special roller foot, or Teflon foot, for use with leather, imitation leathers, and plastic. These feet are designed to glide over materials that may adhere to other feet. Use very thin leather for appliqué. A long straight stitch or a wide zigzag can be applied without splitting the leather.

ABOVE LEFT *The closed bronze doors of* The Tournament *triptych were made from leather, papier mâché, handmade paper and braid.*

ABOVE *The figure in this detail from the* Princess Marigold *quilt has been cut from leather. To avoid splits, it is advisable to use a long straight stitch to apply leather.*

APPLIQUE WITH NON-FRAYING MATERIALS
Its non-frayable quality makes felt a particularly easy fabric to use for appliqué. Try painting it to create unique effects. Felt may be attached to the background by slipstitching along the edges. Felt appliqué is a quick-and-easy method that children can quickly grasp. A scene of felt cut-outs can be quickly built up, and interfacing may also be painted in bold, bright, imaginative colours and used in much the same way. Try stitching some sheer fabrics or nylon stockings over the applied shapes to create other effects. Some of these fabrics can be pinned or glued to the background to hold them temporarily while hand stitches are used to fix them in place. Free machine embroidery can be used to blend the top fabric of the applied piece into the background.

MANIPULATING FABRIC FOR APPLIQUE
Special fabrics may be created by burning, ruching, stitching, or any other technique that alters the usual look and feel of the fabric. Most synthetics will singe along the edges and bubble under the direct application of a naked flame; other fabrics might burst into flames, so take great care and always begin by testing a small sample piece, placing it in a saucer. Fabrics can be pleated or sculptured through gathering stitches, and altered in many ways.

APPLIQUE WITH FUSIBLE WEBBING

Any number of surface fabrics may be applied to the background fabric with fusible webbing, which is marketed under a large number of trade names. Read the manufacturer's instructions for the method of using this webbing, but experiment with sample pieces.

Small bits of fabric and thread may be applied in a profusion of colour and texture with the same webbing. Try using a background fabric of vanishing muslin or hot-water-soluble fabric. Apply bits of fabric and thread with fusible webbing. Using free machine techniques, work machine lace over the whole, connecting all of the applied pieces, then dissolve the background fabric according to the manufacturer's instructions. When you have finished applying the bonded pieces, continue with other techniques.

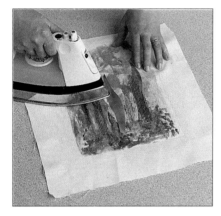

1 For the background, transfer the chosen image, in this case an iris, to the heavy cotton background fabric, using transfer paints. Paint lightweight silk and net, and then back them with fusible web. Cut the leaf and petal shapes from this bonded fabric. Carefully position the leaf and petal shapes on the background and iron them to fuse them to the background.
Three-dimensional effects may be created by bonding only a small part of the shape, allowing part of it to stand out from the background.

2 The fairy has been attached by another method. Trace the fairy's shape to a piece of light cardboard and cut it out. Cut a piece of 56g (2oz) batting to fit the card shape and attach it to the card with a light application of glue. Cut a piece of lightweight jersey or nylon stocking to the shape of the fairy, leaving a 1cm (⅜in) allowance to turn under. Place the fabric over the card and batting, turn the edges under, and secure the edges to the back of the card with glue. Make the clothing slightly larger than the figure so that the edges may be turned and glued to the back of the card. Outline any desired features with flesh-coloured thread. Make hair from fine silk. Slipstitch the figure to the background fabric.

ABOVE *The* Iris Fairy *was created by Julia Barton in the tradition of Shakespeare's fairies in* Midsummer Night's Dream. *It combines a fusible webbing background with applied padded shapes and both hand and machine stitchery. Size: 30cm × 26cm (12in × 10½in).*

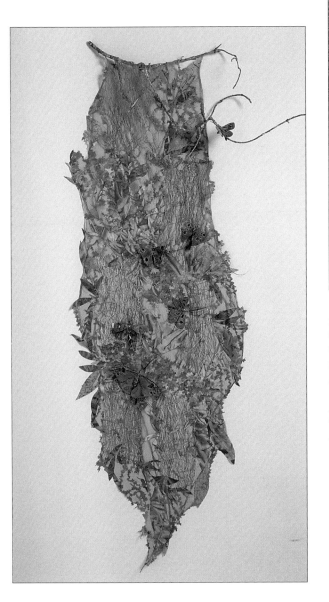

LEFT *Jane Hall created the background for* Where Fairies Gather *by working machine lace on a dissolving fabric. Over this she fused many flower shapes. The panel incorporates a number of hand stitchery techniques, and hangs from a tree branch.*

ABOVE *Three-dimensional butterflies and moths were worked by hand. Couched gold threads were used to support the applied details.*

TURNED EDGE APPLIQUE

One of the most traditional appliqué methods involves turning under the edges of the applied shapes. The turning prevents the edges from fraying and increases the durability of the article. Traditional hand quilters would often make tiny stitches around the edge to apply shapes to the cover fabrics for their quilts, leaving the appliqué as the outstanding feature of the work.

The edges of appliqué shapes are normally turned under if the shapes are going to be applied by hand stitches, and the shapes should be simplified as much as possible. This technique is very useful when applying manipulated or padded fabrics to a background.

Fabrics made from natural fibres, especially cotton, are easiest to turn. Lightweight interfacings, cut to the exact shape of the design (without turnings) and ironed on, can be a helpful guide to turning edges. When planning shapes, try to match the grain of the background and appliquéd fabrics.

RIGHT St George and the Dragon, *by Dorothy Sharman and Barbara Oborne, is chiefly formed from appliqué and patchwork. St George and his adversary were first padded with batting; the edges were then turned under, and were slipstitched to the green background. Size: 163 cm × 102 cm (64 in × 40 in).*

ABOVE The Firebird, *by 9-year-old Emma Nichols, was inspired by a Russian fairy tale of the same name. Emma traced the figure to a white background and, after a rummage through her mother's scrap fabrics, quickly cut some brightly-coloured fabrics to fill the shapes of her design. The edges of some of the applied pieces were turned under, but others were left as they were. Beads and sequins were liberally added with simple hand stitches. Size: 26 cm × 20 cm (10 in × 8 in).*

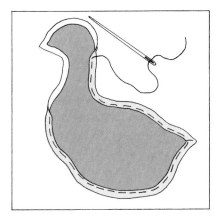

1 If you are backing the shape with an interfacing, take a paper pattern or the design tracing and draw the appliqué shape on the iron-on interfacing. With a warm iron, press the interfacing on the back of the fabric. Leaving a 6mm (¼in) allowance all around, cut out the shape. Turn the seam allowance over the interfacing on the back, and baste around the shape.

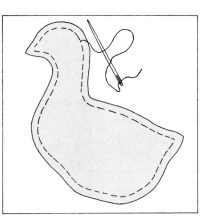

2 Sometimes, iron-on products would stiffen the fabric too much, making it unsuitable for its intended use. If this is the case, trace the shape directly on the fabric. Add the seam allowance, and cut out the shape. Sew a basting thread around the perimeter of the finished shape. This will act as a guide when you turn the edges.

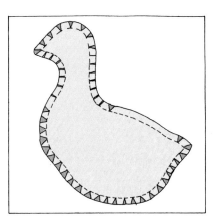

3 To facilitate turning the edges on outside curves, cut a few 'V'-shaped notches in the turning, close to the finished outline. On inside edges, cut a few slashes vertical to the outline. Do not cut into the interfacing or basting stitches.

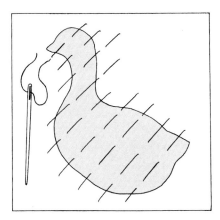

4 Set the background fabric in an embroidery frame, centring the area to be appliquéd. Taking care to match fabric grains, pin the appliqué piece to the background fabric. Baste the shape to the background fabric. Basting stitches should go through the main body of the shape and not on the edges. The basting is necessary to prevent unwanted puckering of fabric during appliqué stitching.

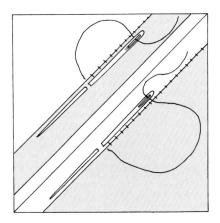

5 Slipstitching should be almost invisible. With a threaded needle, pick up as small an amount of fabric as possible from the background. Slip the needle into the turned edge of the appliqué shape, taking as little fabric as possible, and back into the background fabric, again taking up a small amount of fabric.

MACHINE QUILTED APPLIQUE

Textile artists use a number of different methods for the creation of appliqué. Linda Straw uses a method that incorporates appliqué and machine quilting with machine satin stitch. She has mastered this technique to perfection with her highly individual way of working. Her emphasis always on the story, she conjures up images of the characters in her mind before tackling the drawing.

The photographs show a very simplified version of Linda Straw's work, but it would make a good starting point for anyone who would like to try this method. Experiment with other variations to achieve different effects. The layers of fabric may be added singly or three or four at a time.

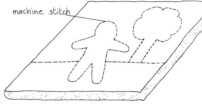

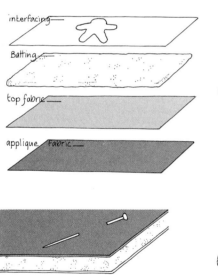

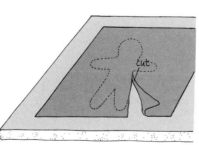

1 The cartoon is traced or drawn on interfacing (not the iron-on type). Make a sandwich of the interfacing (tracing facing out), batting, and an outer layer of lightweight ground fabric. Add a piece of fabric of the selected colour over the area that is to be appliquéd. All corners are then pinned together.

2 Set up the machine for free running stitch, and sew through the material sandwich, over the area where the coloured fabric was positioned, working from the interfacing side. The shapes must be fully outlined with stitches. The stitches around the edges should be shorter than the normal length. Turn the work over and cut away the excess fabric.

3 Continue to apply coloured fabrics over design areas and outline them from the interfacing side of the work. Change fabric colours as required, cutting away excess fabric as stitching progresses.

LEFT *This detail from the* Romeo and Juliet *quilt shows the star-crossed lovers. Linda Straw has established herself as a teller of tales through quilting, and has developed an individual approach to appliqué.*

ABOVE *As if directing his play, Shakespeare oversees the production of* Romeo and Juliet *as it unfolds over the quilt. Notice how colour is deliberately underemphasized in the background details, in order to draw the attention to the main characters.*

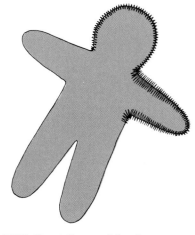

4 Reset the machine for automatic satin stitch. Working on the front, work satin stitch around all the edges of the design elements, changing stitch width while sewing, to suit the design. Add any other machine embroidery to the front.

ABOVE *Juliet's tragic end at the bier of Romeo brings the tale of the feud between the Montagus and the Capulets close to its finale.*

BELOW *Queen Mab is the midwife of dreams – the mischievous fairy who produces the dreams of men.*

RIGHT *Linda Straw draws the entire design – full size – on interfacing, and then assembles the interfacing, batting and silk background fabrics. Working from the interfacing side, she stitches the outlines of the design, at the same time applying coloured fabrics in their appropriate places to the quilt front. Madeira rayon machine embroidery threads are used for the stitching. Size: 274 cm (108 in) square.*

CUT-BACK APPLIQUE

C ut-back appliqué is worked from the front, by cutting through layers of applied fabrics of different colours. This also creates a sculptured look. Layers of fabric are successively cut away until the wanted colour is exposed. You will have to make a full-colour cartoon for the design of the piece; each colour used will necessitate a layer of coloured fabric.

Many contemporary needleworkers and quilters use this technique, though the layers of fabric make the work more bulky to handle than other forms of appliqué. To keep the bulkiness within reason, it is advisable to use no more than three or four layers of fabric (with very lightweight fabrics you may find it possible to have more layers). Felt may be used with this method though it is bulkier than many other fabrics. Felt does not, however, require as much stitching as do frayable fabrics. Consider dyeing a range of colours and layering these together to create more interest.

Free machine embroidery may also be worked on pieces of fabric before they are layered together. Avoid wasting time and materials on areas that will not be visible through the cut-outs or on the surface. To avoid this, make an overall drawing of the area on your cartoon, and trace each shape separately. Lightly trace the outline of the relevant shape on each layer of fabric. The areas of exposed fabric may then be planned to allow work on areas that will show.

After all the shapes have been cut back to the selected colour or fabric, the exposed edges can be treated in one of several ways. Left as they are, they will leave a frayed effect which, if planned, can look very pleasant. Zigzag or machine satin stitch can be applied to the exposed edge of each layer, adding interest and colour. Either hand or machine quilting can also be applied over the layers for a sculptured effect, capturing light and shadow. You can baste a layer of batting to the underside of the work for more effective quilting.

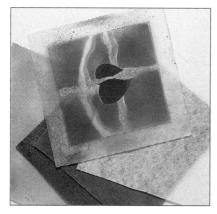

1 Transfer the design to Stitch-and-Tear. Layer each fabric of the required colours under the Stitch-and-Tear, taking care to put them in the correct order for the design.

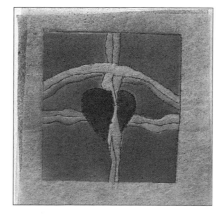

2 Set the machine for very short straight stitch. With the Stitch-and-Tear on top, stitch around all the design areas. Each area must be fully enclosed with stitching. Carefully remove the Stitch-and-Tear.

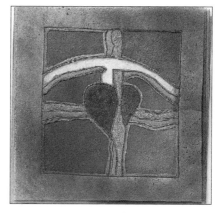

3 Using small, sharp scissors, cut away the areas enclosed in stitches. Referring to the design, cut away as many layers as necessary to get to the desired colour. Satin or zigzag stitch may be applied around design edges if desired. Non-fraying fabrics may not need this additional stitching.

An old fairy tale theme, retold in a story by Pushkin, and related to Linda Straw when she was a child, inspired her to design this cover, entitled Malachite.

The tale is one of love regained through trial and adversity. The maiden (red) has lost her love in the Ural Mountains. Malachite (green), the goddess of coppermining, prescribes to her a number of tasks that she must complete in order to find her lost hero. Note how the figures extend into the borders, giving the impression of leaping out of the frame.

The decoration on Malachite's dress was worked in free and automatic machine embroidery. Note how the satin stitch narrows, widens, and changes colour around the shapes to provide contour and dimension. Linda has used her own special style of appliqué on silk. The cover was loaned by Linda Maltman. Size: 53 cm × 66 cm (21 in × 26 in).

APPLIQUE AND CUT-BACK APPLIQUE

Textile artist Alison Bramley uses appliqué and cut-back techniques, worked in a spontaneous way. She uses heavyweight cotton backing fabric and sometimes chooses blanket fabric as a padding for her quilted work. She has also used other battings, including both cotton and polyester types. In her latest quilt (not shown here) she used silk batting, which is very much lighter in weight, and is therefore particularly suitable for a large hanging quilt. The following are simplified steps to the way in which she has executed her most recent projects, but this could change in the future.

1 Design a full-size, full-colour cartoon on tracing paper. Fasten this to a window or other light source and over it attach a medium to heavy cotton fabric, the full size of the cartoon. The background fabric should be backed with iron-on interfacing. Trace the design on the fabric. Remove the fabric and begin tracing individual areas of the design from the cartoon to a paper pattern.

2 Layer together as many pieces of fabric (silks, nets and other types) as are required to reproduce the colours of individual paper patterns. Transfer the design from the paper pattern to the top fabric. Using free running straight stitch, sew around each design element that you have transferred from the paper pattern. Cut back as many layers as required to get to the desired colour. Stitch around each area. Continue this process until all the main designs of the cartoon have been reproduced on individual pieces.

3 Position each of the individual design pieces on the background fabric. Baste them securely to the background and stitch around the edges of the design outlines. Further appliqué of the background, to tie the individual areas together, may now be accomplished using standard appliqué methods. Appliqué shapes can be added, using either invisible threads or threads that match the colours of the applied fabrics.

The Wizard of Oz was designed and made by Alison Bramley. Size: 240 cm (96 in) in diameter.

CHAPTER IV

MACHINE EMBROIDERY

This section covers both automatic and free machine embroidery.
Automatic machine embroidery is generally described as stitching with the
feed dogs engaged, in other words in the up position, feeding the fabric
through the needle as in general sewing. For free machining, the feed
dogs are disengaged, or down.

B efore beginning any machine embroidery, always set your machine for a test, adjusting tensions to produce a perfect straight stitch. To thread your machine, put the presser bar in the up position. This will open the tensioning system. Thread through the guides; wind the bobbin with a thread of the same size, but of a contrasting colour. Bring the bobbin thread to the sewing surface. Place a piece of fabric under the needle and lower the presser bar. Set the top tension to the middle point (usually 3 to 5).

Sew a line of straight stitch. Remove the fabric and check to see that none of the bobbin thread shows on the front of the fabric and none of the top thread shows on the bottom. If the top thread shows on the bottom, gradually increase the top tension in small increments until the top thread no longer shows on the bottom of the fabric. If bobbin thread shows on the top of the fabric, gradually increase bobbin tension until the bobbin thread no longer shows on the top of the fabric. It is essential for machine embroidery to be able to adjust top and bobbin tensions. Read your manual and become familiar with the movements of adjustment. Altering tensions will not harm the machine.

Top tension is usually adjusted by a numbered dial. Some machines may only have a + or − indication on either side of the mid-point. Check your manual for bobbin tension adjustments.

Special threads have been developed for machine embroidery. Size ranges from 30 to 50 are suitable for use on the top of the machine as well as in the bobbin. Select the smallest needle that will allow the free passage of the thread without causing it to shred. For most decorative or satin stitches being used for appliqué, use a top thread of the same colour as the top fabric. It may be necessary to change top threads quite often, but if the back is not seen or will be lined, there is no need to change the bobbin thread.

Fabric to which heavy stitching will be applied requires support. Use one or two layers of Stitch-and-Tear under the fabric. Alternatively, an embroidery frame 20 to 25 cm (8 to 10 in) in diameter may be used to support the fabric. The embroidery frame is an aid in turning the fabric to guide it through awkward shapes or corners. Do not try to move the frame back and forth, as in free machine embroidery; allow the feed dogs to feed the fabric.

Foot selection is also important. An open-toe appliqué foot allows a view of the stitches as they form. The satin stitch or embroidery foot has a special groove on the sole to allow thick stitching.

The Forsaken Merman, *by Linda Straw, was inspired by the poem of the same title, by Matthew Arnold. This quilt is worked in an appliqué method perfected by the artist. It has a silk background fabric and silk batting. Satin stitch is worked with Madeira rayon machine embroidery threads. The piece measures 108 cm × 158 cm (43 in × 63 in) and was borrowed from the collection of Susannah Clasen.*

MACHINE TENSIONS FOR SATIN AND DECORATIVE STITCHES

N ew domestic sewing machine technology has put in the hands of home users a greater capability than could have been imagined a few short years ago. Most new models will produce a satin stitch that could formerly only have been produced on commercial machines. The greatest aids to satin stitch versatility are the abilities to produce very wide stitches and to alter the width and length of the stitches. Many machines will produce a standard satin stitch 6 mm (¼ in) wide. The computerized Pfaff can be programmed to produce a satin stitch 9 mm (⅜ in) wide. Regardless of the machine, however, it is still impossible to produce a professional-looking satin stitch unless the instructions below are followed.

Adjust the top tension so that the bobbin thread is not pulled through to the top surface of the fabric. The bobbin thread should not be seen on the edges of any decorative stitches. If the bobbin thread shows on the surface, either reduce the top tension or increase bobbin tension. Most machines will require a reduction of top tension. Unless the work will be viewed from both sides, a small amount of top thread showing through on the back of the fabric will not matter. If the back is on view, use a thread of the same colour on the top as in the bobbin.

MAKING AN EVEN SATIN STITCH

It is sometimes difficult to get good, even coverage of the fabric with satin stitch. Allow the feed dogs to feed the fabric normally. If a firm backing is used, the fabric should flow through the needle without pushing or pulling over the feed dogs.

The size and characteristics of the top thread will dictate the stitch length. Adjust the length to get the desired coverage. Fine threads will allow closer stitches, and you should always use machine embroidery threads. If the stitch length is set too short, the stitches could be too close to each other and the needle may jump back over preceding stitches and stop the machine. Older machines may have this tendency, but you can correct it by length-

ening the stitch slightly. When the stitch length is correctly set and stitches are forming, run the machine at a constant speed, with minimal starting and stopping.

The control that regulates stitch length is set for small incremental changes, so when you make this adjustment, move the control in small steps. Try a number of different settings. Close attention to these tips will be the best guarantee of a beautiful, well-formed satin stitch.

ZIGZAG AND OTHER AUTOMATIC STITCHES

If satin stitch is difficult to conquer on your machine, or if it does not suit your fabric or design, there are other stitches available. A narrow zigzag or other decorative stitch can be an alternative.

APPLIQUE WITH ZIGZAG AND SATIN STITCHES

Always relate the width of the stitch to the size of the piece being applied; the smaller the piece, the narrower the stitch width should be. Narrow stitch widths also make it easier to turn corners and follow intricate shapes.

Satin stitch may be narrowed, widened, or tapered by adjusting the width control. On most machines, this may be done during stitching. Begin the satin stitch with the needle just over the outside

edge of the piece to be applied. Most of the stitch should form on the applied piece. At the beginning and end of the stitching, move the stitch length control to '0' and work a few stitches in place to secure the stitches. Backstitching with satin stitch should be avoided; instead, the top thread can be taken to the back and tied-off with the bobbin thread.

Interesting variations to satin or zigzag stitches are created by winding the bobbin with a thread of a contrasting colour to the top or with a metallic thread. Adjust the bobbin tension until the bobbin thread shows through on the front of the fabric. Try threading two threads of different colours through the needle.

ABOVE LEFT *A scene from* The Forsaken Merman *shows happier times. The mortal mother, Margaret, is combing her child's hair while seated upon a throne deep under the sea. The detail of the satin stitch around the appliquéd figures shows the contouring effect.*

LEFT *The merman searches throughout the seas for his beloved Margaret.*

ABOVE *Mortal Margaret is applied with satin stitch. Her hair is modelled with Madeira rayon machine embroidery threads. Free running stitch is used to describe her facial features.*

QUILTING WITH APPLIQUE

I t is possible to combine several techniques on some quilts. Fairy tale images may be appliquéd and then machine embroidery may be used to decorate shapes. One of the quilting methods that I like to use allows me to appliqué with satin stitch before I quilt.

After all of the appliqué has been finished, the quilting lines can be established. Make a sample to confirm choices of stitches, techniques and effects. The sample will usually expose any problems that you might encounter while working the piece. Be sure to baste all layers firmly together to allow the article to be worked and manipulated as a single piece.

This will give you the freedom to move the piece rhythmically under the needle.

Some quilting lines may be worked inside the outlines of the applied pieces. These lines may be planned to pull the composition together. Always stitch quilting lines from the centre of the piece, working outward in all directions. This reduces the chances of puckering the fabric, because any excess is eased to the outside edges. A lining over the back of the work is sometimes advisable in cases where tied-off threads and puckers may show on the back of the work. For functional items that may see a lot of wear or need washing, use dressmakers' threads which are

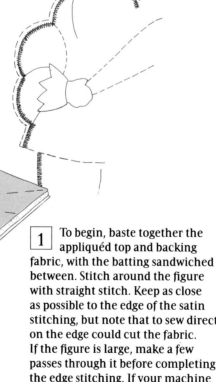

1 To begin, baste together the appliquéd top and backing fabric, with the batting sandwiched between. Stitch around the figure with straight stitch. Keep as close as possible to the edge of the satin stitching, but note that to sew directly on the edge could cut the fabric. If the figure is large, make a few passes through it before completing the edge stitching. If your machine has a dual feed, or walking foot, engage it; this feeds the top fabric, and helps to prevent the layers from shifting.

2 Plan the pattern that will be formed by the lines of quilting so they contribute to the tale being depicted. The lines may outline background features or echo the central figure or theme. Try varying the distance between lines, so that some are together and others are wide apart. If there is any doubt about how this will look on your piece, make a pencil drawing before adding stitches.

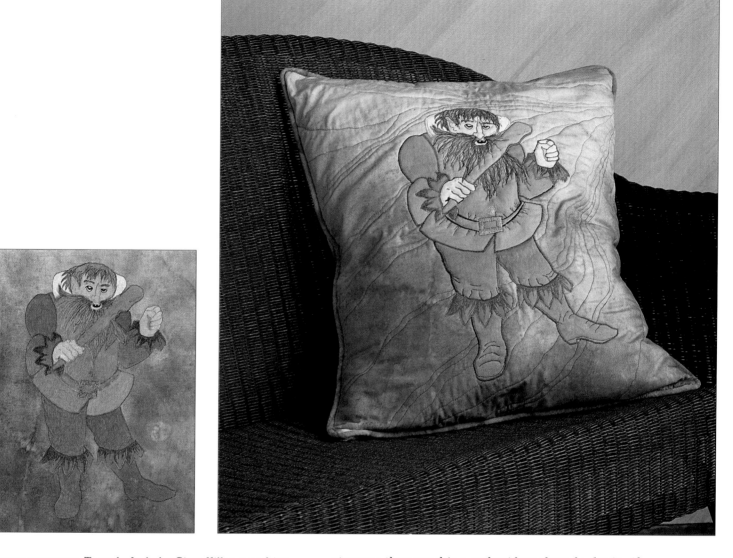

ABOVE AND RIGHT *To make* Jack the Giant Killer, *a cushion cover designed and executed by Cecile Damon and Gail Harker, Jack was first painted on cotton fabric by Cecile. A purple wash was applied to a cotton background fabric, to which Jack was appliquéd, using the whole-piece method. Free machine embroidery was applied while the piece was in a frame. Satin stitch was worked over the piece. The prepared cover was laid over batting and machine quilted. Thread colours were chosen to blend with the background. Size: 46 cm × 51 cm (18 in × 20 in).*

stronger than machine embroidery threads. Again, if the item is to be used functionally, follow the quilters' rule of keeping quilting patterns no larger than a fist. This will help to secure the batting from moving around inside the piece. If the item is to be used in a less functional way, the lines may be planned to be more decorative and will not require such close spacing.

Quilting with automatic stitches can be very difficult on large pieces; it is not easy to turn corners and follow patterns with so much fabric under the foot. The stitch length should be set to 3–4 mm (⅛–⅙ in), to accommodate the bulk of the fabric.

FREE MACHINE EMBROIDERY AND QUILTING

While the roots of embroidery can be traced back over the ages, machine embroidery owes its existence to the industrial revolution and the invention of machines for stitching. These machines radically reduced the labour required to create sewn products. They also enabled the artistic to create patterns and develop techniques that are still in use today.

Free machine embroidery came into its own as an art form in the 1920s and 30s. Unfortunately, the swing needle machine had not been invented at this juncture. Machine embroidery pioneers produced works of art with straight and zigzag stitches. They also recreated traditional embroidery techniques, such as drawn-thread work, hedebo, point de Venise, and Tenerife wheels, to mention just a few.

We have in common with the pioneers the need to learn the coordination of the movements of the embroidery hoop and the needle. We call this 'drawing with a needle'. Modern swing-needle machines allow us to select stitch widths and lengths and let the machine do the work, swinging from side-to-side, producing an even zigzag or satin stitch, and opening up a new world of artistic expression.

Free machine embroidery is one of the subjects not generally covered in machine manufacturers' manuals, though the general principles are sometimes discussed under 'Darning'. Free machine embroidery may be adequately accomplished through the use of only two stitches – zigzag and free running stitch. The skill that has to be developed is to combine foot pedal pressure (sewing speed), and embroidery frame movement under the needle to create a variety of stitches. The frame may be moved in any direction – forward, backward, diagonally, or in circles.

The free movement of fabric under the needle demands the disengagement, or lowering, of the feed dogs. This is easily accommodated on some machines through a special control, but on other machines a cover is available. This must be placed over the feed dogs and properly attached (see the instruction for your machine). Free machine embroidery may be done with no foot attached, but I always advise using the darning foot supplied with the machine.

Set your machine for straight running stitch, with both the width and length at '0'. The top tension will usually need to be reduced. Place the presser bar in the down position, and remember that the stitch length is now controlled by the sewing speed and your movements of the frame.

Free machine embroidery may be used either to outline areas (as with a pencil) or to fill in areas (as with a paintbrush), as well as for quilting and appliqué. In most cases, the fabric is held in an embroidery frame; this is because it must be held firmly, to resist unintentional puckering, skipped stitches, and breaking threads, during machining. However, a frame is not necessary if the fabric is sufficiently firm or stiff to allow free movement.

STIFFENED FABRICS

Fabrics can be stiffened for frameless embroidery by applying heavy starch or roller-blind (window shade) solution. These additives may be removed by washing, but the stiffness will also be reduced as you work, and the fabric will soften. The ideal method is to combine the stiffened fabric with a layer of batting and a further layer of stiffened fabric under the batting. This sandwich must be basted together so that it reacts as a single piece of fabric. The multi-layered fabric will produce a much more even stitching and resist puckers. Be creative, and experiment with individual effects. You might, for example, try using interfacings, organdies or felt.

While stitching on stiffened fabrics, your hands

The Princess and the Pea was designed by Gail Harker. Colours were chosen for each of the mattresses, and fabric was dyed to match. Free machine embroidery was worked on each mattress and on the princess before they were applied. Size: 135 cm × 203 cm (52 in × 80 in).

will perform the same function as the frame. Hold the fabric firmly to the bed of the machine, closely framing the sewing area with the fingers. Your hands will then guide the fabric under the needle to create your own personal and unique design.

THE QUILTING

Quilting can be done with either free running or free zigzag stitches. Satin stitch could also be used, but this must be stitched at a slower pace. Free machine quilting offers the freedom to create the beautiful flowing lines that are not possible with automatic stitching, because the fabric can be moved in any direction rather than being restricted to forward and backward motions.

A piece as large as a single-bed quilt may be worked on the machine. Given a little patience, larger pieces may be accomplished, but I find that to stitch pieces larger than single-bed size is very tiring, entailing the pushing and pulling of large amounts of fabric.

Use a transfer pencil to work out the general lines of quilting on the top fabric. One of the important keys to success is to be sure to baste all fabrics together before machining.

As fabric colours change, many thread changes will be required. Secure threads by sewing on-the-spot, by reducing stitch length and applying several tiny stitches, or by backstitching. I like to use a combination of dressmakers' threads (size 50) and machine embroidery threads for satin stitch.

The quilting should be balanced over the area of the quilt. I use some of my quilting stitches to pick out elements of the design, such as floor tiles, arches or doorways. Detail is difficult to obtain on batting heavier than 56g (2oz). Quilts and large embroideries can be rolled up so that they fit between the arm and bed of the machine. Unroll the work as you progress.

Machining can be made easier if you construct the quilt in sections that are pieced together, jigsaw fashion, when the work on each piece is completed. The divisions may be strategically placed along natural lines of the design. The dividing lines need not be horizontal or vertical, or even straight, but should match up to the adjoining pieces. Draw lines on your cartoon to indicate logical divisions.

ABOVE *The mattresses were appliquéd to a background fabric large enough to contain all of them. Batting was placed under this and free machine embroidery was worked over the top. The stack of mattresses was then applied to the background in one piece.*

Another way to approach the problem of constructing large pieces is to make a central panel of more manageable size. Around this, design a series of borders that can be added to the quilt in individual bands. This can be built-up to almost any required size. Another way of adding borders around a central block is to build them up in a squared spiral, as in log-cabin style.

THE MAKING OF THE PRINCESS AND THE PEA

The Princess and the Pea quilt was made in several stages. First, I drew the full-sized design on a piece of interfacing, and then traced paper patterns for all of the shapes I had decided to appliqué. A heavyweight cotton fabric was chosen as the background fabric. To this I added a wash of paint, trying to effect a granite colour.

The appliquéd pieces were made of white cotton and a polyester-silk blend. These were dyed with Deka L to the colour scheme that had been developed. The dyeing process for several colours on 20m

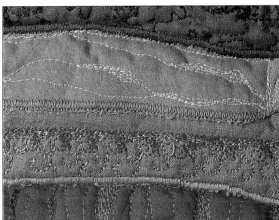

LEFT *Care was taken to use dyes that could be fixed to make them colourfast and withstand cleaning.*

ABOVE *Mattresses were individualized by using decorative stitches over each one. Programmed stitches were combined with free machine embroidery.*

(22yd) of fabric should be spread over a number of days. Heat setting the dyed fabric, when a long length is being processed, can be eased by the use of a flat bed presser, such as the Elna Press. The large surface of the presser and the ability to apply weight to the fabric simplifies ironing.

The stained-glass windows were applied first, using the whole piece method. It was necessary to dissect them into manageable sizes.

Mattress patterns were traced on the fabric of the selected colour. These were cut from the fabric, numbered for easy indexing, and placed on cotton sheeting (unbleached muslin) with the mattresses outlined upon it. Under the cotton sheeting, a layer of 56g (2oz) batting was placed. I then basted the individual mattresses to the cotton sheeting, taking the stitches through the batting.

Free running stitch was used to outline all the mattresses, and a free machine pattern was then applied to each mattress to give it some individuality.

The firmness of the two fabrics and batting allowed this work to be done without a frame. When this was completed, the mattresses were basted to the background. They were then appliquéd with free machine stitches to their allotted place. Excess fabric was then trimmed away from the applied piece. Next the figures were applied, by the whole-piece method.

A large piece of batting was placed under the background fabric once all of its applied work had been attached. The batting was securely basted to the background fabric. Free satin stitch was used to outline each of the mattress shapes.

To finish the quilt, I collected pieces of the dyed fabric used for the mattresses and cut them into narrow strips. These were stitched together on mediumweight interfacing to form a long ribbon of coloured strips. I determined a border width and calculated the intersection of the corners, which were then mitred. The whole border was stitched to the quilt.

DRAWING WITH THE NEEDLE

One of the concepts that become apparent after you are familiar with free machine embroidery, is that the needle may be used in the same way as a pencil.

Drawing with the needle is similar to putting pencil to paper or brush to canvas. One can freely sketch by eye or follow designs that have been previously applied to the fabric. Free running stitch may be used both as an outline stitch and as a filling stitch.

Use the smallest frame that is practical and the smallest needle size that will accommodate the thread and fabric.

It is advisable to use a firm, heavy cotton or upholstery fabric. If lighter fabrics are desired, it may be necessary to stiffen them with additional fabric, interfacing or fusible interlining. Ensure that a sufficient border has been left around the design to allow it to be framed.

Once you appreciate the enormous range of applications and the freedom of creative expression that is possible with free machine embroidery, you may be driven to develop your skills. If you feel intimidated by the prospect of taking a piece of fabric and attacking it under the full flow of creative juices, first draw or trace a design on the fabric. Practise following the lines of the design and add any variations imposed by the moving spirit.

Cable stitch is another of the very decorative stitches that can be applied with machine embroidery. Free cable stitch is used to add heavy threads, giving a three-dimensional feeling and texture. Hand embroidery threads, or other heavy threads are wound onto the bobbin. (Bobbin tension will need adjustment to allow the free flow of thick threads.) The stitch will form on the underside of the fabric, so be sure to turn the work face down. While machining, you will only be able to see the top thread. Set the machine for free running stitch, and stitch as for any straight stitch.

RIGHT *The scenes on this* Alice in Wonderland *tablecloth, by Christine Barlex, were inspired by the illustrations of Arthur Rackam. Designs were transferred to the cloth using the prick-and-pounce method. Free running and zigzag stitches were used to draw the scenes on heavy upholstery fabric. The cloth was loaned by John Gordon. Size: 226cm × 150cm (89in × 59in).*

LEFT *The Mad Hatter presides over the tea party, which is attended by Alice, the Hare and the Dormouse. 'I see what I eat, I eat what I see', the writing contained in this scene, was stitched with the drawing-with-the-needle machine embroidery technique.*

MACHINE LACE

Machine lace can have all the delicacy of hand lace but can also be very sturdy. You can create lace to any design of your choice, using these steps as a guideline for your cartoons. Many different patterns may be created for machine lace, and free running stitch is used for most of these. The threads must intersect each other in order to create a supporting network of threads. For stronger, heavier lace, retrace the lines of stitching many times.

Solid lines represent solid stitching. It is essential to think small and work out ideas for patterns before machining starts. Practise following lines and patterns on spare fabric before stitching the main piece.

Hot-water-soluble fabric allows very dense stitching and added layering of other fabrics. The

1 Begin by drawing the design or object on paper. Make a heavy outline in coloured pencil. Using your coloured pencil, dissect the shape into more manageable small segments. These lines will represent the bars into which you will be stitching. Choose a variety of patterns to fill in each of the shapes.

2 For a background, draw a regular shape (rounded or rectangular) around the design or object. Fill the surrounding area with repeat patterns. These may be squares, boxes, stars or circles, for example. Interconnect all of these shapes with a network of lines worked from each solid shape. The designs do not need to be followed meticulously, but will be a guide to the type of pattern desired.

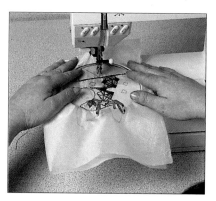

3 Position your design and fabric on a bright window. With a pencil, lightly trace the basic shapes and outlines on your fabric. Frame two layers of fabric. Using free running stitch, outline all the areas where bars have been drawn. Be sure to stitch over these areas a sufficient number of times to achieve the strength required to support the weight of the threads that will be added. Referring to the paper pattern, begin filling in some of the patterns.

fabric may be worked either with or without a frame, and cable stitch may be applied. Zigzag stitches may also be applied, but be sure to stitch over the zigzag with two or three lines of straight running stitch or the zigzag will unravel when the fabric is dissolved.

After the stitches have been worked, place the work in a pan of gently boiling (simmering) water for about five minutes or until the fabric is dissolved. The work will appear to be shrivelled up, but do not despair. Rinse it under warm flowing water, and after rinsing, place the work on a dry towel laid on a board and gently stretch and shape the piece, pinning it to shape and then leaving it to dry naturally.

Due to the sturdiness of hot-water-soluble fabric, larger amounts of fabric may be worked than with other soluble fabric. When it is necessary to make lace to fit a particular shape, it may be beneficial to work a series of small pieces, assembling them to fit the measurements. Additional dimension may be achieved by adding stitches to the edges.

Vanishing muslin is another useful material upon which to support machine lace while stitching. After applying stitches, press the piece with a hot iron until the muslin turns a dark black-brown colour. Heat may be applied in an oven set for 200°C (400°F). Lightly brush away the charred muslin.

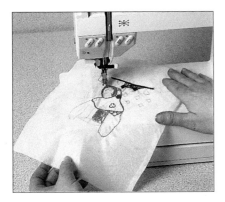

4 To alter textures in some of the work, apply small pieces of fabric (use fusible web) to the soluble fabric. Stitch over these pieces. To finish the work, reset the machine for automatic satin stitch. Ensure that a network of many straight lines has been applied to support the satin stitch. Apply satin stitch. The satin stitch may be further supported by sewing a line of straight stitch on either side. Dissolve the supporting fabric and remove the residue.

Princess Ludmilla is one of the principal characters from Pushkin's narrative poem, Russlan and Ludmilla. *Free machine embroidery was worked over dissolving fabric. After the figure was complete, the supporting fabric was dissolved, leaving the lacy figure. Size: 14 cm × 22 cm (5½ in × 8¾ in).*

LEFT The Wicked Witch of the West *is born of the luminous Kansas sky and* The Wizard of Oz. *Bea Sewell formed this vision of the nemesis of Dorothy and her companions from a padded shape, to which scraps of ragged and burnt velvet, silk and other fabrics were applied. Size: 42 cm × 53cm (16½ in × 21in).*

ABOVE And Shall I Reach the Stars? *is an unframed panel by Chris Barlex, who is inspired by English fables and fairy stories. The great fish, seeing the rainbow of stars, attempts to get his passenger to them. The whole panel is deliberately worked without a frame in free zigzag stitch. This creates an intentional buckling and contortion of the fabric under the tension of the stitches.*

FREE MACHINE EMBROIDERY AND AUTOMATIC STITCHES

H ighly decorative stitches can take the centre of interest away from the basic design idea. Unless the stitches are intended to be the focus of the design, it may be advisable to use invisible embroidery thread (usually monofilament nylon) on the top of the machine. This specially-produced machine embroidery thread has sufficient strength to support the weight of most embroidery and quilts. You will probably need to reduce the top tension.

Machine embroidery thread of a colour matching the background will also tend to blend in and be less visible. It is well to remember that machine embroidery threads lack the strength of ordinary dressmakers' threads. Use them for decorative purposes, but where strength is required, revert to dressmakers' threads.

During the Victorian era, when patchwork was at a peak of popularity, the focus of attention was generally directed toward the threads. Patches of various materials and of all sizes were placed on a backing. A wide variety of hand stitches were worked in a glorious array of colour over the joins between the patches. Similar patchwork may be achieved by incorporating machine embroidery, using some of the many built-in stitches available on most machines.

RIGHT *Alison Bramley incorporated nearly every element of the classic tale in her* Sleeping Beauty *quilt. The witch is in the top corner, with Sleeping Beauty, Prince Charming, the castle tower, and the good fairy spread around the quilt. The principal technique used was cut-back appliqué, most of the stitchery being in invisible thread. Size: 183 cm × 92 cm (72 in × 37 in).*

LEFT *The wicked witch is depicted in cut-back appliqué.*

Apply any fabric to a background. To protect individual pieces against fraying, go around the edges with a straight automatic stitch, using a monofilament nylon (invisible) thread. Keep the stitches close together; this will create a misty feeling over the area. You might use free straight stitch, creating a design, or doodle, as you go, or try automatic zigzag to create other effects. These techniques will add yet another focus of interest to your work.

HINTS ON THREAD USAGE

Certain of the metallic, rayon, and nylon threads will have a tendency to unroll erratically off the reel (spool) and, sometimes, to break. Some machine manufacturers supply a special guide to cope with this difficulty. However, the problem can be controlled by taping a tapestry needle (or other large-eyed needle) alongside the reel, setting it slightly behind and slightly higher than the reel. Thread the machine, first through the eye of the needle and then through the usual thread guides on your machine.

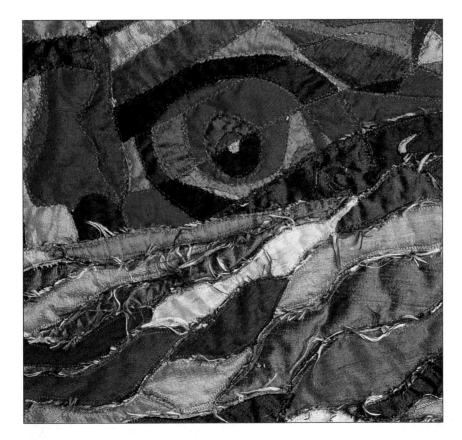

RIGHT *Sleeping Beauty is shown at the bottom of the picture, along with other symbolic elements of the tale.*

LEFT *The working of Sleeping Beauty's tresses can plainly be seen in this detail.*

RIGHT *The chair, trunk and other elephant theme items are by Janet McFarlane Knowles. Inspiration for this assortment of elephant thematic items came to Janet after much research; she found elephant postcards, pictures and books, obtained samples of sari materials, and even went to the zoo to do some sketching.*

ABOVE *A number of thematic motifs were developed by Janet for this border design, collage and embroidered fabric. The border design was intended for use as a frieze; the collage was built up with paper and was covered with white woodworkers' glue. This leaves a plastic-like finish on the paper. The look of traditional arts and handcrafts are the hallmark of Janet's work.*

RIGHT *Using collected design materials, an elephant was painted on a sheet of paper. Sumptuous border designs were developed and placed around the edges. The design study could now be used as a picture, to complement and accompany other items.*

FREE MACHINE QUILTING

Paddy Killer researched her fairy tale, *The Little Mermaid*, at her local library. She acquired two different versions of the story and began to develop design and colour ideas. Using a small drawing to work out compositional ideas and a full-sized drawing to determine the organization of the quilt, she produced her design.

At the bottom of the design, she visualized a setting with a circular garden floating in the sea. Above that, she designed a shoreline, with a ship on the horizon and a stairway ascending to a palace. On each side, over the palace, she designed a semi-circular colonnade with golden domes at the top.

BELOW *The design shapes are drawn on the fabric in blue ink, using a technical drawing pen. Free machine running stitch is used to fill in solid areas between the sea shells on the border.*

BELOW RIGHT *Vermicelli stitch is machined between the arches of the colonnade, creating a textural effect.*

Behind this, she placed mountains and the sky, containing the north star, clouds, and the wind. She placed the Little Mermaid on a pillow, ascending into the sky to be borne away on the winds.

Paddy designs by putting stitches on paper to show the direction and build-up, or space, in different areas. After settling on her design, she creates samples with fabrics, paints, and thread colours.

She has developed her own individual way of working her counterpanes. She sprays the top fabric (silk) and bottom fabric (cotton organdy) with roller-blind stiffener. She draws her design directly on the silk fabric, using a technical drawing pen and permanent ink. The top and bottom fabric are basted together with a thin layer of batting between.

First running stitch is worked around the main outlines. Some areas are then filled with free vermicelli stitch. Pieces are worked in manageable sizes; and are then fitted together, overlapping, and stitched.

ABOVE The Little
Mermaid *was designed
by Paddy Killer as a
counterpane/bedcover
for a single bed.
Size: 146 cm × 246 cm
(57 in × 97 in).*

LEFT *The counterpane and matching cushion cover create a wonderfully coordinated setting.*

VERMICELLI STITCH

Vermicelli stitch has been a favourite of machine embroiderers ever since the machine was introduced. In reality, it is not so much a stitch as a technique, the aim of which is to organize the meandering directions of the stitching lines, and it is used to fill large areas with textural pattern. The collection of the Victoria and Albert Museum, in London, includes an early 18th-century example of a vermicelli stitch flat quilt (a flat quilt being one which consists of a top and a backing with no batting). Back stitch was used to quilt this example, and was generally preferred and used by flat quilt workers. The V&A example also

RIGHT *Paddy Killer designed her* Little Mermaid *cushion to match the counterpane. Sympathetic design elements are carried over to the cushion. The sun and hair are painted on with permanent paints.*

ABOVE *The witch is at the bottom of the counterpane. Free running stitch was machined over the background in dark purple. Vermicelli stitch has been machined around the circle.*

shows the use of vermicelli to create a wandering pattern around the flowers on its silk background.

In her book *Quilting*, Averil Colby describes a traditionally-used and identical pattern, which she calls 'meandering', and it is interesting to note that many of the earliest surviving examples of quilting incorporate embroidery stitches.

Fortunately for me, I have found yet another name for vermicelli stitch or meander pattern – it is called 163 on the range of decorative stitches programmed into my computerized Pfaff sewing machine. At the touch of a button, the computer will instruct the machine to produce this pattern in varying stitch lengths and widths. Previously, free machine embroiderers had to spend a considerable amount of time developing the skills required accurately to manipulate the fabric under the needle to produce this intricate pattern. It is an excellent technique to practise as an exercise to develop free machine embroidery skills.

CHAPTER V

HAND STITCHES
PATCHWORK WITH HAND QUILTING

Patchwork is yet another of those techniques that had their place in
antiquity. Born of necessity, it has been used by needleworkers from the time
the first needle was whittled from a thorn or bone. Earliest man pieced
together bits of hide, and when fabrics were first produced, stitched those
together to make functional items of apparel or protection.

P atchwork flourished in the remote mountains of Appalachia from earliest colonial
times and on the Great Plains of America
during the westward expansion. New fabrics were
extremely difficult to come by, and out of necessity,
every usable scrap was recycled into bed quilts and
items of clothing.

Traditional English patchwork is based on the use
of shaped templates over which the fabric is folded,
and basted, before being joined with overcast (whip)
stitch. To use the traditional method, divide your
cartoon into shapes and make templates. Cut pieces
of fabric to suit the design concept, choosing from a
wide range of monochromatic, polychromatic, or
contrasting colour schemes.

During this century, patchwork has grown into
a major art form. Sometimes it is quilted, using any
of several methods, and at other times it is in itself
a finished piece of art. Running stitch, one of the
simplest hand stitches, is also one of the most
beautiful for hand quilting.

Linda Negandhi, who created *The Frog Prince*,
collects scraps of left-over fabric from a bridal-dress
designer. She then dyes the fabrics with Deka L to suit
her own preference and the needs of the design.
Hand quilting on a frame, she uses Gütermann silk
threads to match the colour of the background fabric.

From the original design for *The Frog Prince*,
Linda drew a full-sized cartoon on paper. The
cartoon was marked out in suitable template shapes.

FAR LEFT The Frog Prince *(backside) in
progress – basting stitches are used to
secure the templates and fabric until
the slipstitching finally joins all the
pieces together.*

LEFT The Frog Prince *(front) in
progress – after all the fabric patches,
to which templates have been basted,
are joined, the paper templates and
basting stitches can be carefully
removed.*

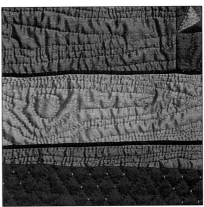

ABOVE The Frog Prince, *by Linda Negandhi, captures the enchantment of the fairy tale: 'The next morning, when she awoke, there he was on her pillow. And then with one leap to the floor – there, before the astonished princess, stood a handsome prince.' Size: 166 cm × 117 cm (66 in × 46 in).*

The shapes were converted to individual paper templates and cut out. Referring to the original design, fabrics of the proper colours were selected.

Each template was pinned to the fabric, taking care to match fabric grain to its intended alignment with the other shapes. Allowing 6 mm (¼ in) extra all around each shape for a turning allowance, she cut out the fabric shapes, and turned the allowances to the back, basting each to its paper template.

She then stitched the templates together with a very small whip (overcast) stitch, using No. 50 dress-makers' thread. Linda occasionally laid the joined templates on the cartoon to confirm accuracy.

When all the templates had been sewn together, Linda mounted the patchwork with the batting and bottom fabric on a quilting frame. Gütermann's silk quilting thread was matched to the colours of the top fabric. Running stitch was used to echo the shapes of the pattern pieces.

SHADOW QUILTING

S hadow quilting and shadow appliqué are exciting ways to translate a collage-based cartoon into a fairy tale creation. One of the popular methods for shadow quilting entails placing brightly-coloured patterns of fabric on a background. This is covered with a transparent fabric, creating a soft, pastel, shadowy effect. This technique lends itself very well to the creation of figures in a fairy tale. Running stitch should be used to outline the shapes and hold them in place between the layers of fabric.

Any type of dressmakers', quilting or machine embroidery thread may be used for the quilting. Threads of contrasting colours applied around the edges of the designs will highlight the stitches. Threads of the same colour as the background will be barely visible, giving the shape more prominence than the stitches.

The background should be a mediumweight fabric that will work with the design. The fabric may be dyed or painted, using techniques described in the section on colour. The figures or cut-outs should be in contrasting colours, and will be easier to work if they are of a fabric that does not fray too much. The shapes could be backed with iron- on interfacing to make them easier to use. The transparent overlay could be chosen from any number of fabrics, including curtain voile, cotton organdy, silk organza, polyester organza, or very lightweight silk. The fabric could be white or a pastel shade. Before quilting, add a lightweight batting and backing fabric.

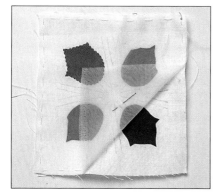

1 Arrange design pieces or figures on the background fabric. A light application of fabric glue, a short burst of spray glue, or fusible webbing could be used to hold pieces in place.

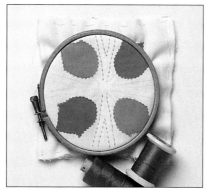

2 Apply a sheer fabric over the top of the piece and mount the assembled fabric, along with batting and backing fabric, in a frame for stitching. If the piece is of a fairly large size, it would be advisable to baste all the layers together before working.

ABOVE *Hilkka Dorey was inspired by European folk tales when designing a quilt for a baby's room. To create the desired pastel effect, the small quilt was worked in shadow quilting. Size: 63 cm × 81 cm (25 in × 32 in).*

LEFT *The Snow Queen is a book panel, made by Diana Dolman for use as one of the pages of her fairy tale book of the same name. The snowflakes in the background are outlined in shadow quilting. Hair and other features are depicted in straight stitch. Over this, sequins and diamanté were added. Size: 16 cm × 22 cm (6½ in × 8¾ in).*

CROSS STITCH

I believe that cross stitch is one of the most versatile of all the embroidery stitches. The true origins of this stitch are lost in antiquity. It must be assumed that it was one of the earliest stitches used to decorate fabrics when regular, even-weave fabrics came into existence, and it is certainly the stitch most universally known to the embroiderer. It has been adopted by almost every ethnic group in the world. It is suitable for canvas or any other even-weave fabric on which threads may easily be counted.

Cross stitch has been known as gros point. Canvaswork (needlework) using cross stitch was known in the middle ages as *opus pulvinarium* (cushion work). Because the stitch is basically described in squares, it imposes a design discipline that tends to be schematic rather than naturalistic.

Europeans have traditionally worked cross stitch in very fine, colourful patterns to decorate clothing. Many European folk costumes are embellished with vast quantities of designs in this stitch.

It is best to work cross stitch in a frame in order to prevent distortion of the background fabric. To develop an even, consistent appearance with this simple, two-step stitch, you must ensure that all top stitches slant in the same direction.

SCHEHERAZADE
The haunting tale of Scheherazade, whose very life depended upon the suspense and excitement of a continually unwinding series of fabulous tales, told nightly to her cruel husband, the Sultan, is the subject of Janet Edmonds' work.

 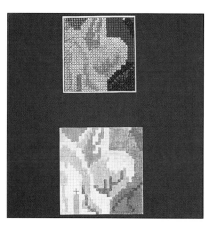 

1 An easy method of applying a grid to original artwork in order to transfer a design is to photocopy a piece of graph paper of the desired grid size on a transparent sheet (overhead slide foil).
This transparent grid may be used over any artwork to create a cross stitch pattern, and then to transfer, enlarge, or reduce the work.

2 Janet produced a colour laser copy, using this type of grid over her full-colour cartoon of *Scheherazade*, forming a perfect pattern for cross stitch. The resulting full-colour copy with grid may be used as the working cross stitch chart. Each square on the grid represents one cross stitch of the colour shown in the square. Grids of two sizes are shown, to indicate differences in the scale of stitches.

3 Look at a range of fabrics for cross stitch. Almost any fabric with an even, regular weave is usable. These fabrics are identified by the number of threads per 2.5 cm (1 in) in the weave. Remember, cross stitch demands that you count those threads, so the fineness of the weave will dictate the type and size of thread that may be used. Very fine weaves will allow you to depict finer detail.

LEFT *Scheherazade was the spinner of tales in the* One Thousand and One Nights, *her very life depending on the suspense element in the stories she unfolded to her husband, the sultan. In this framed picture, entitled* Scheherazade, *Janet Edmond has worked cross stitch patterns from her own design. Aida, evenweave fabric, 18 threads to 2.5 cm (1 in), in navy blue, has been left unworked to show through in some areas. Size: 29 cm × 24 cm (11½ in × 9½ in).*

BELOW *The 18-thread weave of the fabric permits the degree of detail to be seen. For greater detail, a fabric of a higher thread count could be used, or the design could be enlarged.*

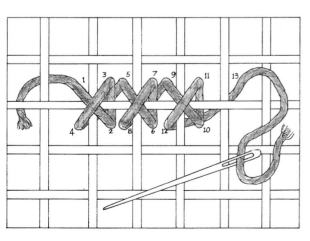

To make cross stitch, insert the needle from the back of the canvas into the starting space (1), and follow the numbered sequence, continuing until the space has been filled. All of the top, crossing stitches should slope in the same direction.

FREE CROSS STITCH

Using different design methods can often lead to inspiration, suggesting new ways of depicting an idea, as well as a novel application of stitches.

The first three steps shown here should be worked concurrently with each other, in order to coordinate shapes and colours.

The section on the development of the cartoon explains some of the techniques used by Janet. A collage was used for the development of one design. She felt that a literal interpretation of the subject matter was less important than to develop a number of figurative ideas. She considers many stitching possibilities from her wide repertoire of embroidery techniques when she explores ideas in drawing media. After the design ideas have been committed to paper, she makes several stitch and fabric samples to test the ideas. This process results in the rejection of some concepts. Finally, a plan of action is laid down.

To achieve the rich textural feel and sensuous colours she was seeking for *Scheherazade*, she decided to place layer upon layer of fabric over and under a grid of canvas. Over this went raised-work

RIGHT *Also entitled* Scheherazade *and by Janet Edmonds, this wall hanging incorporates cross stitch, zigzag on rug canvas, appliqué, free machine emboidery, stumpwork, and some straight stitch. Size: 75 cm × 80 cm (29½ in × 31½ in).*

heads. Free cross stitch was applied at random over the fabric, as was free machine stitching, and all the while she continued to apply scraps of fabric. The result is a very unusual combination of effects.

Textile artists such as Janet have developed a very open attitude to the tactile nature of materials in the creations of their special art form. Using media and techniques from all of the graphic arts, they become not just creators of needlework, but sculptors, painters, weavers and knitters, as well as embroiderers. The art stands on its own merits.

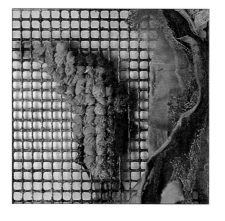

1 | Janet started with a purple cotton background fabric. Large appliqué pieces were cut to shape and pinned to this.

2 | Rug canvas was spray painted with automobile spray enamels. Some areas of the canvas were worked in cross stitch, using threads made of dyed fabric torn into strips.

3 | The heads were painted separately. Scrim was laid over the heads and machine embroidery worked over the top.

The partially-worked rug canvas was laid over the background, followed by the heads. To provide relief, the heads were stuffed and stabstitched to the other fabrics.

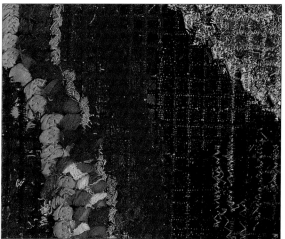

ABOVE *The detail from* Scheherazade *shows how disparate techniques can be combined in a single work. Here, underlying fabric may be seen through the canvas. Machine zigzag is worked over the layers of fabric, including the canvas, attaching other strips of fabric.*

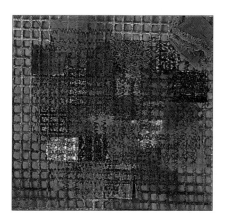

4 | Machine zigzag was worked in some areas over the figures, after these had been applied to the rug canvas. Many small squares of fabric were laid on the background to enrich its texture, and these were blended in with free machine stitches.

5 | The border was knitted. Shapes were then applied with both hand and machine stitches. The border was strengthened with batting and backing fabric. Metallic gold powder, applied by sponge, was used for the printing.

CANVAS EMBROIDERY

C anvas embroidery has been practised throughout Europe since medieval times. One of the oldest canvas stitches, tent stitch is particularly durable and hard wearing, and lends itself to the interpretation of detail. Worked in a frame, this stitch should be executed in two motions (up and down), rather than in a single scooping motion.

A variety of canvases and threads are commercially available. Normally, any canvaswork thread should fill the space provided and cover the weave of the canvas. If threads of too small a size are selected, the canvas will look very sparse and the weave will show through to the surface. Threads that are too thick cannot be worked without distorting the canvas. You must also take care to use a tapestry needle that will carry the thread through the available hole without stretching and distorting the canvas.

To make her Sleeping Beauty hearth stool, Annwyn Dean selected interlock-mono canvas,

number 12, for her design, which she traced onto the canvas, using permanent black ink. To put more detail into the shape of Sleeping Beauty herself than into the surrounding work, she selected a number 18 canvas and traced on it the Sleeping Beauty figure. This was mounted in a separate frame and worked with DMC Perlé number 5 and DMC Rayon, and with Madeira gold and silver metallic threads. The stitched canvas was then frayed up to the edge of the figure.

She folded the frayed threads to the back of the figure and taped them down. The shape was then positioned on the background canvas and secured to it with stab stitch, applied around the perimeter of the figure. The surrounding background was then finished, using tent stitch. Three strands of Broder Médicis (crewel) wool was threaded in the needle and worked on the canvas up to the edges of the figure.

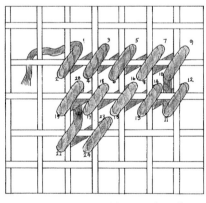

Tent stitch is worked in a series of diagonal stitches. Insert the needle from the back of the canvas at 1, and continue in the numbered sequence. The stitches should all slope in the same direction. At the back, the stitches will also slope in the same direction, across two threads of canvas.

ABOVE AND RIGHT The Sleeping Beauty, *by Annwyn Dean, was designed for a hearth stool, with a matching cushion. The briar rose that entwines Sleeping Beauty is used to pull the design together. The rambling vine creeps around the beloved Sleeping Beauty, relegated to her castle tower, and flows around the cushion. Size (stool cover): 30 cm × 70 cm (12 in × 27½ in).*

BRIAR ROSE CUSHION

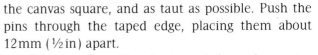

I t can be tempting to stitch with the canvas in your hands, but anything larger than a spectacle case will suffer from distortion unless it is placed in a frame. The distortion can be so great as to make the finished work unusable for any practical purposes. The frame need not be an expensive purpose-built embroidery frame; it could be a simple, home-made, wooden frame. Even a discarded picture frame can serve the purpose.

Prepare the canvas by cutting it to size, leaving a mounting allowance of 5 cm (2 in) around each side. Bind the edges with tape. Sew a basting stitch horizontally and vertically through the centre of the canvas. This will correspond to the centre lines on the grid paper. Bind the edges with tape and lay the canvas on the frame. Try to plan it so that the canvas pulls just short of the outside edge and you do not constantly snag your fingers. Secure the canvas to the frame with drawing pins (thumb tacks). Try to keep

the canvas square, and as taut as possible. Push the pins through the taped edge, placing them about 12 mm (½ in) apart.

Counting from the chart, work from the centre lines outwards. First, tent stitch over the roses and briars, then fill in the background stitches. When you have finished, remove the embroidery from the frame.

A piece that has been stitched in a frame may not require blocking (damping and pinning out to stretch it back into shape). The size of the finished canvas could be the same as that of the finished cushion. If a larger cushion is desired, this can be achieved by applying borders around the canvas (see pages 18-23).

If you wish to develop a design with more personal fairy tale implications, refer to other sections in the book on design development and transferring patterns.

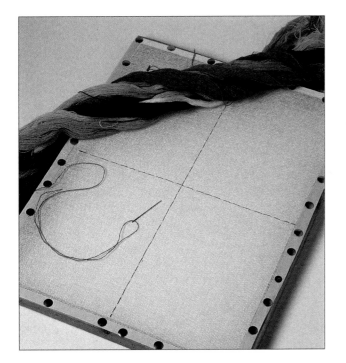

RIGHT Briar Rose, *a cushion cover by Annwyn Dean, was designed to accompany the hearth stool and can be seen on the chair in the picture on the preceding page. The cushion cover was made with single thread interlock canvas, with 10 threads to 2.5 cm (1 in), using four strands of Broder Médicis wool in the needle. Size: 29 cm (11½ in) square.*

Each square on the canvaswork grid represents one stitch. The wool used was Broder Médicis, and the following colours and approximate number of skeins were used:
1 skein each of 8107 and white
3 skeins each of 8401, 8402, 8403, 8224 and 8225
4 skeins of 8309
5 skeins of 8223 and 8877
8 skeins of 8380 and 8381

LEFT *Canvas has been stretched and attached to a homemade frame, ready to begin stitching.*

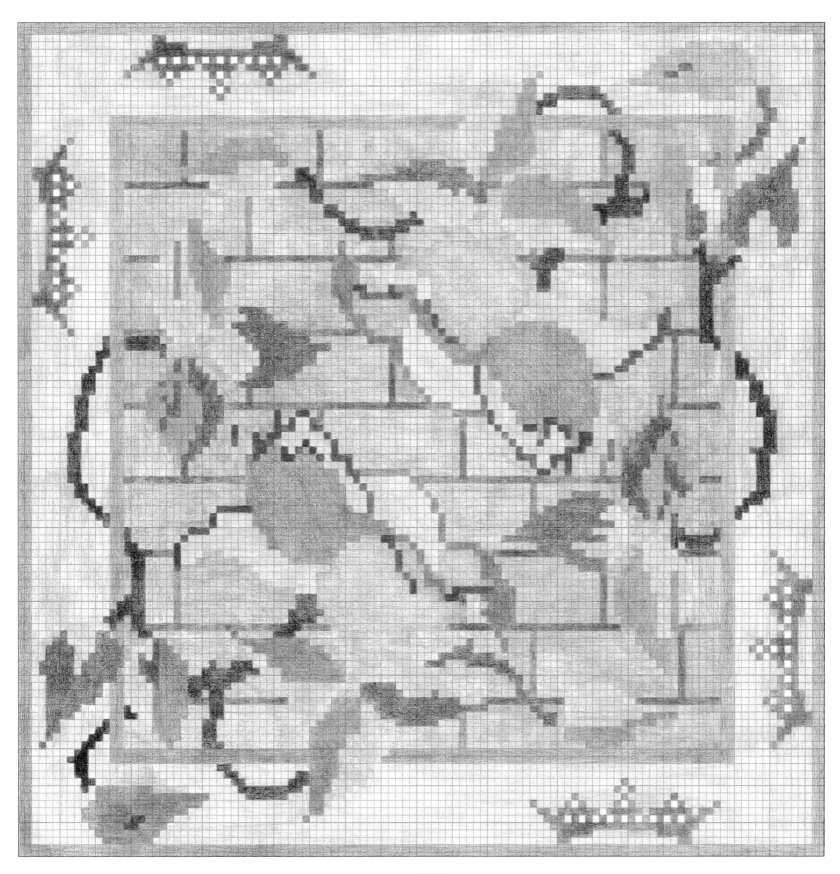

HALF CROSS STITCH

H alf cross stitch looks similar to tent stitch from the front, but is not as durable. Ensure that all stitches slant in the same direction. From the back, the stitches will all be vertical.

Annie Bradstock had always loved the picture of *Titania and the Sea Nymphs* that had hung in her grandmother's house. Years later, she found it in the attic and decided to create her own interpretation. She transferred the design to tracing paper, making alterations to suit the stitchery, and then to canvas, using light pencil lines.

With such a wide variety of products on the market, it can be confusing to try to work out the type of canvas and thread you might need for any particular project. It is even more confusing when there is no standard measure for the canvas. Some shops sell canvas according to the number of holes per 2.5 cm (1 in) and others by the number of threads to the same measurement. But the actual size differences are so minute as to be insignificant.

ABOVE *In this close-up from* Titania and the Sea Nymphs, *it is easy to see the fine detail that may be worked on a canvas with a high thread count. The facial features have been further defined by overstitching with a contrasting thread.*

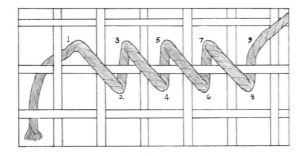

To make half cross stitch, insert the needle from the back of the canvas at 1, and follow through the numbered sequence, continuing until the space has been filled. All the stitches at the front of the work will slope diagonally in the same direction; the stitches at the back will be vertical.

ABOVE *A selection of the many canvas types and sizes is shown, together with some of the many available threads, as follows; DMC Cotton Perlé No. 5 (1) and No. 3 (2), tapestry wool (4), rayonne (5), six-stranded cotton (6), and Madeira six-stranded cotton.*

ABOVE *It can easily be seen why this type of work has often, mistakenly, been called tapestry.*

Canvas should be selected to suit the scale of the work. A number 10 canvas will have either ten holes or ten threads per 2.5 cm (1 in). The higher the number, the more detail you will be able to work into your design. Fine canvases will take longer to cover or will be smaller pieces of work. Canvas with a low number will produce patterns that are very block-like in appearance. Essentially, you will have to choose between single or double canvas, but in general beginners should opt for single canvas.

To get a feel for the many canvases, buy several small samples and try them out. Work a variety of stitches and threads, and keep the samples for refer-

ABOVE Titania and the Sea Nymphs *was worked by Annie Bradstock in half cross stitch on canvas with 24 threads to 2.5 cm (1 in), using three strands of cotton thread in the needle. Size: 47 cm × 116 cm (18½ in × 45½ in).*

ence. Experiment with different thread types and colours. Try combining two or more threads in the needle. In the final analysis, it is your own personal, practical experience that will be the best guide.

The simplest of stitches will often display a design to the greatest effect. A common mistake is to employ too many different stitches in a single work; the best approach is to keep to one or two stitches.

STUMPWORK

S tumpwork is a traditional type of embroidery that reminds one of bas-relief. The technique achieved its greatest popularity in England during the 17th century, when it was also known as raised work. Most stumpwork embroidery of that time depicted biblical scenes, mythological figures, and floral themes. The elements of the scenes were padded to stand out in relief, and the embroideries were used as panels, pictures, and on mirror frames and caskets. Some of the items would be decorated with padded flowers, fruit and human figures. Figures were usually dressed in the costume of the period and set against backgrounds of castles, trees, ponds and animals. The perspective was often curious – people were depicted as large as trees, and insects as big as the people. This embroidery style had all but disappeared by 1700.

Today's artists use stumpwork to suit their own creative ideas, rather than trying to recapture a past period of history. The basic techniques of working with figures and needlelace remain an important part of that old embroidery style, however, and the needlelace figures are applied to the embroidered background. Barbara and Roy Hirst have introduced 20th-century ideas, such as fabric dyeing and machine embroidery, and use modern figures to update the techniques.

This is an ideal medium to create a sculptural representation of a favourite fairy tale. We can only provide a few inspirational ideas and techniques for this enchanting style of embroidery in the development of a simple stumpwork picture, but if you enjoy working in a detailed miniature, this may be the style that will appeal to you.

From the figures represented in the drawing, small portions are selected and drawn separately. These will represent the parts of the design to be executed in relief and will be formed from needlelace. Using a tracing of the artwork, the background is coloured with fabric paint. Net has been laid over this fabric to create an illusion of mistiness. Free machine embroidery is added to create tree shapes and texture. Where the net covers the figures, it is cut away and the figure shapes are padded.

The needlelace pieces are worked on oilcloth. When completed, they are removed and applied over the padded shapes. After the needlelace figures have been applied, individual tree shapes, tree trunks, tree tops, and the tree floor pieces are made from mediumweight cotton, felt and net, backed with iron-on interfacing. These are also applied to the background. It is important to try to achieve a balance of relief between the background work and the stumpwork.

ABOVE *Upper left is the needlelace clothing; at the centre is the painted background fabric, over which machine embroidery has been worked, and at the upper right are the tree shapes that will be applied over the fabric outlines.*

RIGHT Hansel and Gretel *is a stumpwork panel by Barbara and Roy Hirst, evocatively portraying a scene from the story. Size: 19 cm × 21 cm (7½ in × 8½ in).*

OTHER RAISED-WORK TECHNIQUES

The needlelace shapes used to make stumpwork were traditionally called 'slips'. These were often made with detached needlelace, but a wide range of techniques, including canvaswork and other forms of surface embroidery, were also employed. When using any of these techniques for stumpwork, be sure to allow sufficient size to accommodate the thickness of the padded shapes and an allowance to turn under. The finished shapes are then slipstitched to the background.

To pad a shape with felt, cut the first piece the same size and shape as the figure, making additional layers successively smaller. Stabstitch the smallest shape to the background first, building up to the largest. Finally, apply the slip.

All of the needlelace stitches are based upon variations of buttonhole stitch. The *Hansel and Grete* stumpwork shows the use of detached needlelace – corded buttonhole and treble Brussels stitches – for the making of the costumes on the figures.

MATERIALS FOR STUMPWORK

Fabrics For the background, use any mediumweight cotton, silk, or other fabric that does not have a lot of bias stretch. Too much bias stretch can result in puckers around the appliqué. Generally, hand stitches are more easily worked on natural fabrics than on polyesters and other synthetics.

The needlelace stitches must not penetrate the backing fabric. This can be prevented by placing a protective cover of acetate film (contact paper), PVC (vinyl) or architect's linen over two or three layers of mediumweight cotton fabric.

Threads Traditional needlelace was worked with extremely fine threads. Some of these were finer than the finest machine embroidery threads now available. Madeira or DMC machine embroidery threads in cotton, rayon or metallic fabrics; Gütermann silk threads; and single or double threads from stranded cotton can be used successfully. Select a thread size that will create a lace of the correct scale.

Needles You will require a tapestry needle of the correct size, and a sharp-pointed, fine needle.

ABOVE Punch and Judy, *by Rosalind Sunley, is a framed stumpwork picture. Punch, or Punchinello, can be traced back to Roman times, but the notorious hooligan still brings delight to children and adults. Size: 25 cm × 20 cm (10 in × 8 in).*

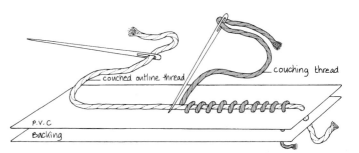

THE CORDONNET

Couching stitch is used to outline the design elements. The stitch is usually worked with two threads. The first is laid along the outline of the design. The second thread is brought up from the backing, through both layers (backing and protective cover), and used to couch down the outline thread, crossing the latter at right-angles. These stitches must be closely spaced to support the needlelace that will be worked to the outline thread.

LEFT *'Curtsy while you're thinking of something to say', the Red Queen tells Alice as they talk in the garden of live flowers in Chloe Percy's framed stumpwork picture,* Through the Looking Glass. *Size: 29 cm × 25 cm (11½ in × 10 in).*

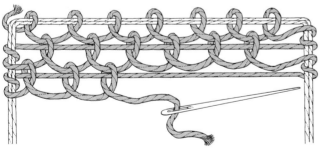

Corded buttonhole is one of the most commonly used needlelace stitches. It is worked in rows suspended from the cordonnet outline to form the needlelace pieces used in Barbara and Roy Hirst's stumpwork.

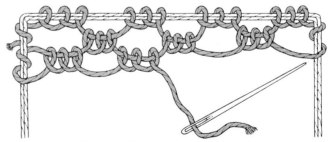

Another popular stitch, and also used by Barbara and Roy Hirst, is treble Brussels. Needlework reference books will indicate a number of other possibilities.

STUMPWORK BASICS

T he steps here show the basic techniques of stumpwork, but there are endless possible variations, some of them described below, for this is pre-eminently an embroidery style in which it pays to experiment. The foundation to support the needlelace is prepared by basting together two pieces of fabric – one of cotton and one of PVC (vinyl), shiny side up. Beginners are advised to start small, with a piece up to about 20 cm (8 in) square.

NEEDLELACE FOR STUMPWORK

Free machine embroidery techniques can be used to make needlelace directly on vanishing muslin or hot-water-soluble fabrics, though machine lace will generally be stiffer than handmade needlelace. The stitches are worked differently, but the effect is much the same. Trace slips or other intricate shapes on any of these fabrics. Apply a cordonnet, or supporting bars of stitching, to the soluble fabric, then make a network of interlacing and overlapping free machine stitches, taking care to overlap the cordonnet on all sides. To release the slip, dissolve the fabric according to the type.

RAISED EFFECT ON FELT

Apply layers of felt to the predetermined shape, then add a covering fabric. Apply machine stitches over the padded fabric; this will create a quilted and raised effect. Additional stitches may be worked

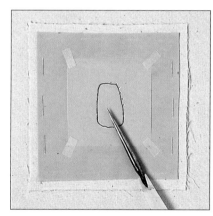

1 Place a tracing paper pattern over the prepared backing materials, shiny side up. Place some padding, such as a folded towel or cushion, under the foundation. Using a needle, prick holes through the pattern into the PVC, following the lines of the design. The holes in the PVC will not heal, which allows the design to remain visible on the plastic.

2 Using the couched thread technique, apply the cordonnet around the design outline, ensuring that the couched thread goes all around the outline, with a small amount overlapping at the ends. Beginning at any edge of the design, stitch all the way across the piece, from one side to the other and back, until you have filled the space with the selected needlelace stitch. Be sure to go under the couched thread on every row at each edge.

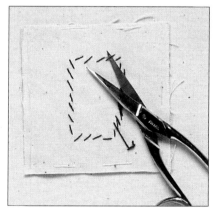

3 When all the needlelace is complete, turn to the back. Using small scissors, clip away the couching threads. This will release the needlelace from the front, so that you can attach it to your design. It may be necessary to pull the couching threads gently away from the back in order to remove the lace.

around the perimeter to blend the raised area with the background.

TRAPUNTO

Quilters have long used trapunto for raised effects, it can even create a stumpwork effect on the front of a background fabric, as with the pods on *Jack and the Beanstalk*. Apply a backing fabric, using either machine or hand stitches to follow the outline of the area to be raised. Turn the work over and cut a small slit through the backing in the outlined area. Carefully insert loose filling, then stitch the slit together.

Machine lace may be used; the outer border and the patterns within the design outline of this piece, made by the author, were free machined on vanishing muslin. The inner square is of hand-stitched needlelace.

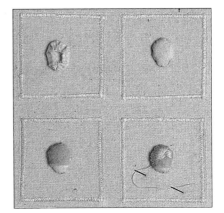

4 From your drawing, trace the forms that are to be padded and applied to the background fabric. This can be done over a light-box or by holding the design up to a window. Use a hard-lead pencil or a disappearing-ink pen. The background can then be painted, adding other details.

5 Decide which elements are to stand out in relief and which are to recede. Cut felt to the size and shape of each piece and stabstitch it to the background, slightly inside the pattern outline. Any parts of the figure that require more relief should be gently padded by adding a little soft-toy stuffing behind the felt. Complete small areas, such as an arm or a leg, one at a time. Next, position the lace pieces over the appropriate areas. Using small neat stitches, attach the edges of the lace to the design outline.

6 Trace the head on a piece of firm fabric, making it slightly larger than the design, to allow for a filling. Baste around the edge of the shape, pulling the thread slightly to gather. Stabstitch the head in position on the background, leaving an opening and adding a little filling through this. To pad out the hairstyle, apply a piece of felt over the appropriate area. Following the natural direction of the hair, make the hairstyle, using straight and other stitches.

HAND STITCHES

L ike Hansel and Gretel, cast into the dark, forbidding forest, Jane Hall, as a child, was also struck with the eeriness of the forest. *Into the Woods*, overpowered by towering trees and grotesque faces peering out of rotting and eroded tree stumps, is the end-product of this inspiration. Using silk fragments and natural materials, such as seeds and small bits of bark, and metallic threads, which she uses for eyes, she intuitively builds her creations.

Beginning at the centre of the piece, she works outward, not knowing how large it will become.

Into the Woods was worked on handmade felt, using long, hand stitches with various combinations of yarns and threads. Some stitches were worked separately on a hessian (burlap) background, to which padded nylon faces, toadstools, and moths were applied. The resulting shapes were then incorporated into the background.

ABOVE The Fairy Ring, *by Jane Hall, is a fabric sculpture in which tiny toadstools are made from silk-covered pipe cleaners, with caps formed by silk discs, stitched together. The caps were padded, and silk fragments were stabstitched to them to create texture and pattern.*

BELOW *For the large stems, circles of fabric were gathered to form a wide base and narrow top, held with wire. Under each cap, fabric was stitched in a funnel and covered with crunched-up fabric. Fabric fragments add further texture.*

ABOVE The face of Gretel peers from the forbidding forest. The faces were made of nylon and padded from behind. Features were stitched over the top.

LEFT Into the Woods, by Jane Hall, features the woods in which Hansel and Gretel were forced to wander. The wall hanging was loaned by Mrs Gillian Pitt-Kiethly. Size: 244 cm × 86 cm (98 in × 34 in).

BELOW *The fragile eggs are made by using fine metallic threads to secure fragments around empty egg shells.*

ABOVE A Nest for Enchanted Jorinda, *by Jane Hall, is a fabric sculpture. The nest is a tangle composed mainly of hand stitches combined with some machine stitching, the latter worked on dissolving fabric and then incorporated into the nest. Feather quills, twigs and ribbons of fabric were woven into the structure. Size: approximately 30 cm (12 in) in diameter.*

ABOVE AND RIGHT The Little Mermaid, *by Jane Hall, is an unframed panel. The silhouetted figure is cut from fine organza, its lower portion being covered in tiny hand-stitched fragments of fabric to create a scaly effect. The hair is made from wisps of fabric and fine thread. The figure stands out about 5 cm (2 in) from the background, which is a mesh of stitches in assorted threads, worked on a dissolving fabric.*

COMBINING TECHNIQUES

F ew expressions of the artistic temperament can match the genius and creativity of the textile artist. Most contemporary textile artists work outside the limitations laid down by art traditionalists; our work demands experimentation with materials and techniques, and we are not limited to a few threads, fabrics, and fibres. Christine Evans enjoyed the freedom to mix and combine a multitude of techniques to express her feelings and impressions in *Cinderella at the Ball*. As it will not be washed, or put to practical use, a picture of this type offers a perfect opportunity to be as creative as possible. This is a medium in which traditional restrictions no longer apply.

RIGHT *The much-loved story of the humble, subjugated step sister/servant, who finds love and fortune through the intercessions of a fairy godmother, is the subject of Christine Evans' framed panel,* Cinderella. *The fantasy of this story is part of the human subconscious – no wonder it appears in some 500 variations, and is to be found in ancient Chinese literature. Size: 43 cm × 81 cm (17 in × 32 in).*

1 Handmade felt provides the background fabric. Individual designs are drawn on Stitch-and-Tear and pinned to the felt. The design outlines are stitched with free running stitch before the Stitch-and-Tear is removed. Curtains and backdrops are filled in with fabric paints.

2 Using fusible webbing, layers of fabric in the shapes of dresses, ruffles, and trousers are attached to the figures. Dyed gauze is applied over the whole panel with fusible webbing. Free machine embroidery fills in gaps and spaces.

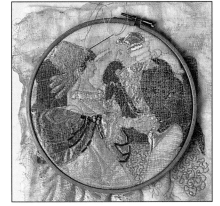

3 To work the fabric, Christine mounts it in an embroidery frame. She then applies straight stitch and French knots over the laid fabrics, adding beads and sequins, to complete the effect.

LEFT *In addition to straight hand stitches and french knots, Christine makes use of a number of techniques, including machine embroidery. The many sequins and beads convey the splendour and glamour of a royal ball.*

CHAPTER VI

FAIRY TALE BOOKS

To my mind, the construction of a special, personal, fairy tale book is the
ultimate means of recreating the wonder and awe of childhood memories.
The tactile qualities of the materials can bring a sense of the eerie, the glitter
of gold and silver evokes an impression of royalty, and the coarse textures
recreate the forest.

C hildren love the sensations that these books bring to the telling of a favourite tale. There is a delicious nostalgia in reliving one's own childhood through the evocation of tales that brought terror, humour, retribution, and the overcoming of adversity. These are the mental images that we can now put to our own creative purposes.

The books may be large or small; they can have many pages or few. What matters is that your book must represent your own special images, different from all others. Book construction could well be a family activity, with something for even the youngest to contribute. As a gift, your book will be cherished by any recipient, young or old.

A combination of techniques may be used to achieve spectacular effects. Glass, rocks, and minerals were the inspirational sources for Barbara Reast in the design of her fairy tale book.

The cover was worked on plain, off-white, mediumweight cotton fabric. This was painted, padded with felt, and appliquéd with a number of other fabrics. Over this, she worked free running machine stitches, and both whip and cable stitch. Satin stitch cord was made and applied by machine. The fabric was then framed so that she could couch threads, sew on beads, and work running stitches by hand. The grid in the centre is canvaswork. A variety of threads were used, including Madeira metallic and machine embroidery threads, Gütermann silk, and DMC hand embroidery threads.

ABOVE *This picture shows the opulent richness created through the use of beads, sequins, and a variety of fabrics.*

RIGHT Aladdin's Cave, *by Barbara Reast, is a book cover. Size: 33 cm × 38 cm (13 in × 15 in).*

THE SEARCH FOR EFFECTS

A collection of glittering threads and other items were needed to create the aura of Aladdin's cave. Barbara worked many samples in her development of the rich, sparkling theme. Beads and sequins are generally available from sewing shops. Other beads could be made from readily available household items, such as soda straws. plastic tubing, or rolled paper or fabric.

ABOVE *Cable stitch cords have been applied to leather and organza.*

ABOVE *In these samples by Barbara Reast, the top left fabric is covered with round and bugle beads and sequins. At the centre are handmade beads – some are made from painted and thread-wrapped metal washers or rings; cotton bead balls (used for tassel-making) are covered with painted fabric, and plastic tubing is painted and wrapped with threads. On the right are painted cotton bead balls. Hand-painted fabrics have been wrapped around knitting needles or skewers, and beads have also been used.*

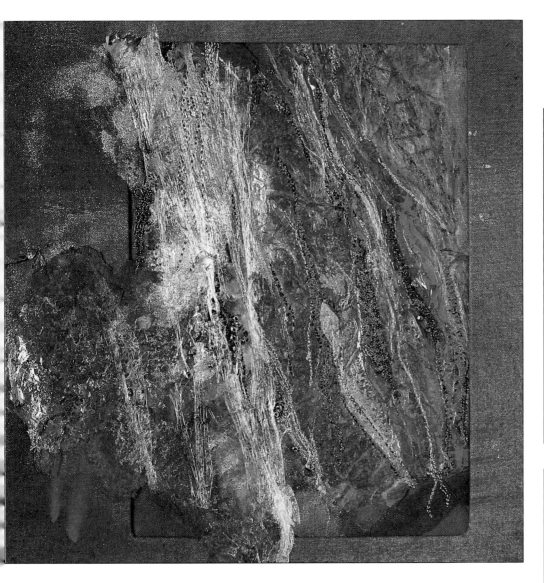

ABOVE *Handmade paper and tissue has been glued to a background fabric and free machine embroidery has been worked over the top. Over this, plastic kitchen wrap has been laid and carefully melted.*

ABOVE RIGHT *Satin stitch cords are made by machine. Centre a cord under the feed dogs and work zigzag or satin stitch over it. Here, cords have been couched to a background made of appliquéd fabrics. Over all of this, running stitches were added.*

RIGHT *Layers of fabric have been applied to the background and free machine embroidery worked over the top. Cable stitch and cords were also applied, to add to the rich textural effects.*

ABOVE The Pied Piper of Hamelin, *by Jean Clarke, is a fairy tale book cover. The elders of the rat-infested town have summoned the piper. Contract discussions are underway,* *to determine how many guilders the piper is to be paid. The excited townspeople are peering through their windows to see the outcome of the negotiations.*

TOP *The piper begins his enchanting tune. Mesmerized rats emerge from every nook and cranny to follow the piper.*

ABOVE *The rats follow the piper. He leads them down to the river where they drown, while the townspeople watch the piper's performance in reverence and awe.*

ABOVE *The Pied Piper, having eliminated the rats, returns for his payment, but there has been a change of heart, and the people renege on the agreement.*

ABOVE LEFT *The piper revenges himself by mesmerizing the children of Hamelin with his haunting tune and leading them away to a cave.*

ABOVE RIGHT *The sad little lame boy is not quick enough to keep up, and the cave closes before he can enter.*

AN HEIRLOOM BOOK

The 'family silver', a term referring to a treasured collection of silver handed down from generation to generation, has passed into the language to mean anything of great real or sentimental value that is held within the bounds of the family. Perhaps future disputes over last wills and testaments will concern custody of that treasured family heirloom, the fairy tale book that you have created. The staggering prices raised by illuminated medieval manuscripts at art and antique auctions are not due to any great intrinsic value that they may possess, such as embellishments of solid gold or jewels, but to their great artistic value. There is no reason why your fairy tale book will be any less valued in centuries to come.

Many of the surviving books of medieval times are decorated with embroidered bindings. Some of them have bindings in which ornate gold-work, precious and semi-precious stones and pearls are attached to beautiful velvets and silks. So precious are some of these books that they are held in environmentally-controlled areas to safeguard them from the elements and the handling of the unappreciative. Some of these volumes may be viewed in museums, just for inspiration, but you will note that they are heavily protected, and you might consider making a special padded book-bag or other container to safeguard your creation.

A fairy tale book will mean something different to each individual who considers such a project. A story can be told on a few story-boards, loosely held in a binding. It could be a series of artistic interpretations that fold up, accordion-style. The tales could be told in purely pictorial formats, or there might be lines of text with each picture. The book could have symbolic figures known only to you and the recipient of the book – that would keep them guessing in the years to come!

The size of the book is immaterial. It could be a tiny volume or large enough to perform the function of a dressing-room screen. The book could be arranged to tell an unfolding story or just depict your own individual impressions of a few scenes from your favourite tale.

Modern sewing machines are often programmed with a number of different type styles. If yours has this capacity, it will painlessly etch out in stitches any words you would like to add.

A treasured family heirloom to be passed on to her grandchildren was the goal of Jean Clarke, and the traditional tale of the Pied Piper of Hamelin was the tale she chose to recreate in her book. She had strong visual images as she mentally reconstructed the story. Deciding on five to six story boards, she drew a design for each one.

Working from her drawings, she painted background, buildings, and other features with acrylic paints on mediumweight calico (unbleached muslin). Foreground figures were cut from cardboard and covered with fabric before being applied. Some figures were padded, using the trapunto technique, to give them an extra dimension. Background figures are simple appliqué. Note how the objects in the distance recede, due to diminishing size and hazy colours.

The applied fabrics include a wide range of wools, silks, velvet, muslin, felt, leather, corduroy, gauze, and, in fact, anything she could apply. A variety of stitches were used to emphasize design areas and add decoration. Jean used couching, running stitch, detached chain stitch, and machine embroidery techniques. Faces were created in stumpwork, with hair formed from wool, silk threads or fleece. Rats were made of applied black wool and fleece, with features picked out with embroidery stitches.

The story board shows the Pied Piper under construction, with padding added to his figure. The buildings in the foreground were worked separately and applied to the background. On the left is the paper pattern for a building, while on the extreme left are photocopied enlargements and reductions of the piper pattern. These were made in order to get him in proportion to the rest of the scene.

FIGURES FOR FAIRY TALES

C reating figures for fairy tales is quite straight-forward. There are numerous techniques which the embroiderer can use to create representational figures. The poses in which the figures are fixed will indicate action or repose. The relative size of the figures, and their position on the background, will indicate depth and perspective.

It was not until the middle ages that artists began to realize that the head of a child was larger in proportion to the rest of the body than that of an adult. As a result, many old paintings show children looking like miniature adults. The usual proportioning of the human figure uses the height of the head as the standard measure. Embroidered figures will probably not contain a lot of fine figure detail, and most of what you need could come from clothing catalogues, children's colouring books or other readily-available sources. Most of these will have action poses of all kinds that reproduce exactly the action you require for your story. Many of these sources will also have animals of all varieties and in all states of action.

Use simple stick figures to compose your cartoon. These may indicate position or, if appropriate, a state of action. Over these positions, the figures can be built-up in the desired costume or attire. Be observant. Notice the relationships of knees to hips, arms to chest and shoulders, and the tilt the body takes when in action. Also try to notice the scale of the surroundings in relation to the size of the figure. If the figure of Saint George is too large in proportion to his horse, he could look as if he were trying to ride a dog.

HEADS AND FACES

We now know not to get the head out of proportion to the rest of the body, but with most embroidery, unless one is making a very large portrait head, it will be very difficult to indicate finely-detailed features. A general head shape will probably be all one can expect. On this shape, tiny features could be picked out with a

few hand stitches. Do not make the mistake of trying to add too much detail.

BELOW *The classic standard for the overall height of the adult figure has been established at 7½ heads: measuring from the top of the head down, the centre of the breast is at 2 heads, the naval at 3 heads, the crotch at 4, knees at 5½, and the soles of the feet at 7½. Giants, titans, and other super-beings will usually be around 9 heads high, the head being smaller than normal in proportion to the rest of the body. Children and babies will have larger heads, with heads proportionately larger in younger children. Grotesque or dwarf figures may have a larger-than-usual head in proportion to the body.*

Notice the relationship of the facial features to each other and their relative positions on the head. Hats, helmets and other headgear do not rest on the top of the head, but usually come down over the head, nearly to the level of the eyes. Notice that eyes are not at the top of the head; they are, in fact, just above the centre line. Actually, facial features occupy a space approximately the size of the hand. If the small features are placed in the correct relative positions, they leave a good impression, even without details.

HAIR STITCHERY

Many artists experience trouble in representing hair. The figures shown in this book have hair created through a range of techniques. Take a closer look at hair in photographs, or on the heads of associates; while we tend to describe people as having blond, brunette or red hair, the fact is that hair is a multi-coloured topping.

Collect as many shades as possible of embroidery thread, hand and machine, of one colour. Use all of these while stitching hair, changing shades as you go.

Paint the background for the hair in the colour desired. Over this, apply small strips of fabric, using fusible webbing. Couch heavier threads and wool, one strand at a time, over the area designated for hair. Arrange the threads into strands and patterns. Use free running stitch to attach threads randomly. You can also add small pieces of hair, made with the machine lace technique on dissolvable fabrics.

Use free running stitch repetitively over the area, building up a texture. Be conscious of the direction of stitches with regard to the pattern of the hair. Use free running satin stitch in the same way, or lay satin stitch cords over the area and attach them with zigzag stitches.

LEFT Rapunzel, Rapunzel, Let Down Your Hair, *by Barbara Reast, is a fairy tale book cover. The beautiful Rapunzel, locked away in the tower, is inadvertantly discovered by a passerby who falls in love with her. The tower has been stitched with machine worked whip stitch and free running stitch. French knots give texture to the moss. The hair is built up of different weights of Madeira metallic threads. Size: 33 cm × 38 cm (13 in × 15 in).*

ABOVE *The six pages tell the tale of a huntsman who was promised a magic cloak that would transport him to anywhere he wished and gold would be deposited under his pillow each night if he shot one of nine birds perched in a tree and removed its heart. The tale includes a bad old fairy and a beautiful young maiden, and as with almost all fairy tales, good triumphs and the huntsman lives happily ever after with the beautiful young maiden. Size: each page measures approximately 7 cm × 13 cm (3 in × 5 in).*

RIGHT The Wishing Cloak and the Salad, *by Cynthia Jackson, is a tale in a bag, concerning a magic cloak, a huntsman, and a young maiden. The story is illustrated with a book of six pages, a bird, a bag of gold, and a magic cloak, all of which are contained within the bag.*

STORYBOOK TEXT

A picture may be worth a thousand words… but a few words can often impart a thousand pictures. Words can inspire fantastic mental imagery that can never be recreated in pictures, and while the books described here are very graphic, the addition of a few lines of the story can enhance the telling of the tale immeasurably.

A line, a paragraph, or a title can be added to almost any pictorial representation, and there are many ways in which this can be done. Some sewing machines, usually the computerized ones, have programmes that will automatically produce as much text as may be required for any picture. One of the problems with these programmes is the small size of the stitched words; some machines will allow the enlargement or reduction of the programmed letters, but the largest sizes will still be relatively small.

Another option is to use stencils, which can be purchased from any school or stationery supplies shop and are available in many sizes. Stencilled words can be worked out and painted on a fabric. These can then be emphasized through outline stitching or other decoration.

Many graphic art books contain samples of various type styles. Trace or photocopy these in any arrangement of words, enlarging or reducing them to the size required. Graphic artists use a wide variety of letters in many type styles and sizes. Commercially

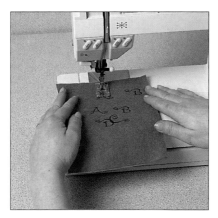

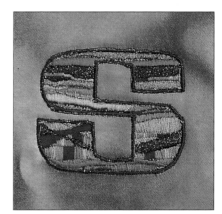

1 Draw a few light pencil guide lines on the fabric. Mount the fabric in a frame or stiffen it. Set the machine for free machining to draw with the needle. Write or print the words directly on the fabric.

2 Many of the newer computerized machines are programmed with one or more styles of lettering. Most are programmed for the alphabet of the country in which they are sold. Following the manufacturer's instructions, programme the letters to produce the desired lines of text. These may be automatically produced on the fabric. Always test the text on a piece of scrap material before committing it to a piece of completed work.

3 Whole-piece appliqué is particularly suitable for applying letters. The applied text may be decorated with hand or machine stitches. The cut-back appliqué method may also be used to create words or letters. The background fabric can be decorated with stitching and colourful fabrics. Baste a layer of fabric over the top. With free machine or automatic stitches, outline the letter shapes. The insides of the letters are cut back to expose glorious ranges of colour beneath.

RIGHT *Margaret Swain used tea and diluted fabric paint to give the look of old parchment to fine linen when making this story book page. The Pfaff Creative 1475 CD has a special digitizing pad called the Creative Designer. With this accessory, individual patterns and letters may be designed and programmed for automatic production by the machine. Using the Creative Designer, Margaret designed each of the gothic letters and programmed her machine to produce the fairy tale text. Other decoration was applied, using computerized decorative stitches available on the machine. Size: 22 cm × 27 cm (8¾ in × 10½ in).*

produced sets of letters are arranged on plastic sheets with a wax coating. The letters may be transferred to paper by merely rubbing over the letter with a stylus. After transferring the desired letters to paper, trace them on fabric and stitch over them. These letter sets are available from most art supply shops.

The computer graphics programme is another source of lettering for fairy tales. Almost every graphics programme will offer a variety of type styles. These may be enlarged to almost any size, reduced, mirrored, and made to follow a line, either straight or curved. The text may be composed on the computer screen and, depending upon the printer, can be printed on paper, fabric, interfacing, or soluble fabrics (see pages 12–13). Some printers will even print colour. After printing the text on your chosen medium, work any stitching technique over the letter.

You might also try your hand at free machining text. Using the drawing-with-the-needle technique, you could manipulate your framed fabric to write out the text you desire.

ILLUMINATED LETTERS

P art of my remembrance of the fairy tale books of my childhood is the striking beauty of the wonderfully illuminated letters that were often used at the beginning of chapters or tales. This practice can be traced back to Byzantine times, and came to the fore in the painstakingly decorated manuscripts of the middle ages. To the monks who spent months copying those books by hand, the additional decoration of illuminated letters, and sometimes whole pages, added immeasurably to their aesthetic value. Illuminated letters have long been used by embroiderers, and perhaps an illuminated letter or two would enhance your own fairy tale.

Measure the area you wish the letter to occupy. Transfer the measurement to a piece of fabric and design the special letter. You can use any hand or machine embroidery techniques to decorate the letter, and you might choose some of the luxurious metallic threads that are now available to simulate the gold and silver leaf used in days of old. Fill in the background area with leafy or floral motifs.

The techniques used by June James include appliqué with padded leather, laid gold work, brick patterning, laid imitation jap goldwork over string, burden stitch, straight stitch, and net overlays. Among the materials used are sequin waste, star-shaped sequins, and beads. Size: 25 cm × 30 cm (10 in × 12 in).

The illuminated letter 'L', by June James, has been worked in traditional or nué, a goldwork technique, in this case with a machine-stitched cord couched over the top. Size: 6.5 cm × 9 cm (2½ in × 3½ in).

BELOW Pamela Smith chose a Cyrillic Pi. The design is outlined in heavy chain stitch over Russian drawn ground. The outer edges are worked in Russian drawn and overcast fillings, and the latter in point Russe and cross stitch.

VARIABLE SATIN STITCH

I sometimes wonder what the pioneers of machine embroidery might have given for one of today's swing-needle (zigzag) sewing machines. But even if it was more difficult, they managed to produce beautiful machine embroideries. They could produce a satin stitch on machines that we now consider antiques. The technique demands great accuracy of hand movement on the part of the machinist, so practice, therefore, is the key to proficiency.

Bear in mind that the longer the throw of thread, the greater the play of light from the surface. Embroiderers have traditionally used this attribute as they planned their stitches. Changes of direction, as well as padding or raising the stitches, catch and reflect light in exciting ways.

FREE MACHINE SATIN STITCH

1 Draw a cartoon on paper and divide it into manageable sizes for the satin stitch. Establish the lines between which satin stitch will be worked.

Transfer the cartoon to your prepared fabric. In this instance, the cartoon was transferred to Stitch-and-Tear, which was then basted to the layered fabrics. Either frame the fabric or layer it to make it thicker. Set your machine for free machine embroidery (free running stitch). To guide stitch production, work the stitch back and forth between the lines of the design.

2 Lightly depress the foot pedal to create one stitch and retract the needle from the fabric. Move the fabric to the next needle penetration point, and, again, take a single stitch. Continue until the area is filled. The machine is run at a very low speed.

STORY BOOK CONSTRUCTION

T here are a number of ways to construct a fairy tale book; I will describe one method that lends itself to embroidered books. Bear in mind that an embroidered page is generally thicker than paper and will require spacing at the spine.

Plan the covers to be slightly larger in size than the pages. The front cover may be highly decorated, but because the book is normally displayed lying on its back, keep the back cover reasonably smooth. For the front cover, use thick, stiff cardboard. A sharp craft knife and metal ruler or straight-edge are essential for accurate cutting.

1 Measure the size of the pages and add the desired amount of cover overhang. Transfer the measurement to the cardboard and, with the grain of the cardboard horizontal to the book, carefully cut two covers. Check the pages to be inserted into the book and make a measurement to the left-hand margin, where the pages will be bound. Transfer this measurement to the covers and make a straight, even cut to separate the back hinge/binding strip.

2 Glue polyester batting or other padding material to the outsides of the covers, and also to the hinge strips.

3 Lay the covers, batting side down, on the back of the cover fabric, keeping the weave of the fabric parallel with the edges of the cover boards. Stretch cover fabric over the inside of each cardboard section and securely lace into position.

4 Measure the height and width of the hinge pieces. Cut the fabric to double the width, plus 7.5 cm (3 in) for an attaching flap. Add a small seam allowance, top and bottom, to the height.

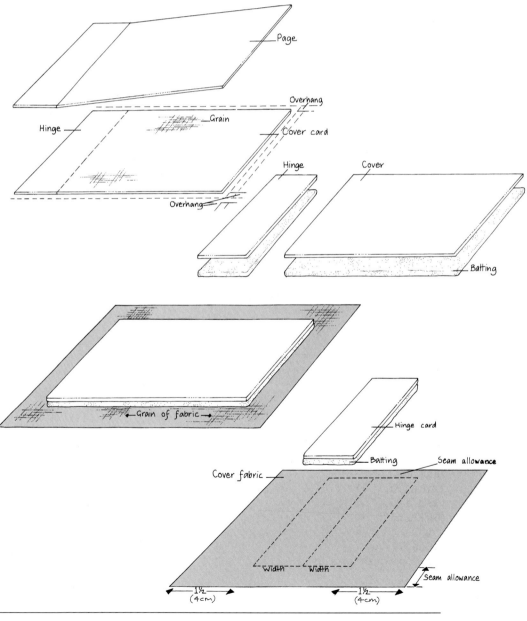

5 Fold the fabric in half over the hinge piece, and stitch as close as possible to the edge of the hinge piece, leaving the attaching flap allowance on one side. Turn the top and bottom ends under and stitch.

6 Turn the hinge piece and cover to the back, and position them with a small gap between to allow for bending. Securely tape the hinge flap to the cover, using fabric tape. Stitch the hinge-attaching flap to the turned cover fabric.

7 Glue a piece of felt or other thin padding over the back of the cover, excluding the hinge piece. The felt should be slightly smaller than the cover. Cut a piece of fabric large enough to line the cover and hinge piece plus a small seam allowance. Position the lining on the full cover and slipstitch all around the inside edges of the cover.

8 Turn the cover to the front and bend back the hinge. Carefully ladderstitch the exposed hinge-attaching flap to the front cover fabric. Use a thread of the same colour as the cover fabric. The stitches should not be seen.

9 After completing both front and back covers, use an eyelet punch to make two holes through the hinge pieces for the binding cord. If you cannot find metal or plastic eyelet rings of the correct colour, the rings may be painted to match the fabric. Punch binding holes in pages and protect them in the same way.

10 Lay the pages inside the covers and measure the maximum thickness of each page. The book will have a neater appearance if each page has a fabric-covered spacer of this thickness, cut to the same width and length as the hinge pieces. Assemble the book by passing cord through covers, pages and spacers.

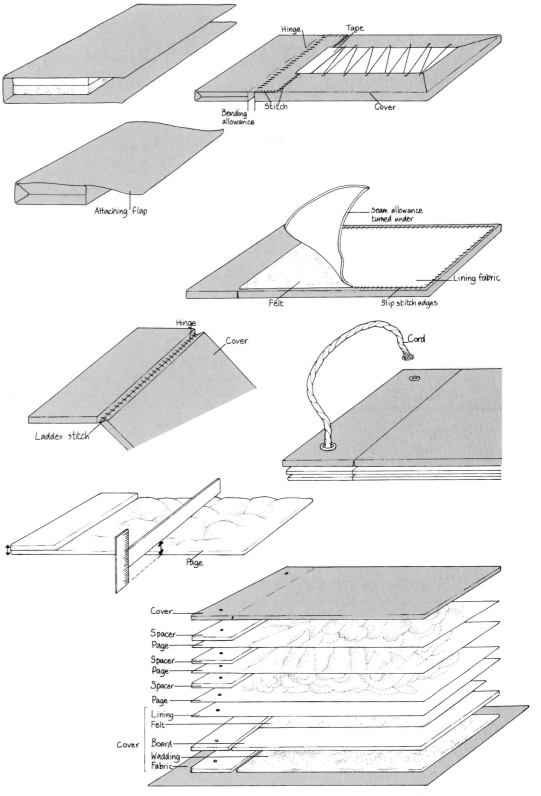

LEFT AND BELOW Jorinda and Jorindel, by Cynthia Jackson, is a wall panel. The story, found in the Grimm collection, tells of salvation through love. Cynthia worked zigzag stitches over coloured felt and other fabric to produce the haunting and mystical atmosphere. Size: 115 cm × 105 cm (45 in × 41 in).

ABOVE The Hans Christian Andersen story is illustrated through needlework in Diana Dolman's version of The Snow Queen. The queen's arms encircle the book to make an impressive clasp. She is made of padded leather applied to a velvet covering material, and her hair and lacy dress were created by applying machine embroidery over soluble fabric. When the queen's hands are unclasped, the book opens to disclose several embroidered pages, depicting scenes from the tale.

FRAMES AND BORDERS

ost of us spend long hours perfecting the designs for our embroideries and quilts, and the borders that frame them should be given as much care and consideration. Borders should enhance and frame the main work, showing it to its best advantage.

1 Well-fitting borders require accurate measurement of the quilt or other work. If the border is a very complex design, it could be made entirely separately from the quilt and added later. Borders may be built up on a backing fabric, with all the strips sewn to it.

2 The length of the border should be calculated by adding the length of the side to twice the border width. To this, add a little extra to allow for the fitting and manipulation of the design at corners. The top and bottom borders are cut to the width of the finished work and attached before the side strips.

3 To mitre a corner, lay the borders in position on the quilt, so that they overlap. Pin the borders in place. With a straight-edge, draw a diagonal line at the corner, from the inside intersection of the borders to the outside intersection. Fold the top border strip over, exactly on the line, and draw a corresponding line on the underlying border piece. Remove the borders and place them with right sides together, aligning the drawn lines, then stitch. Repeat this at the remaining corners, then apply the border to the quilt in one piece.

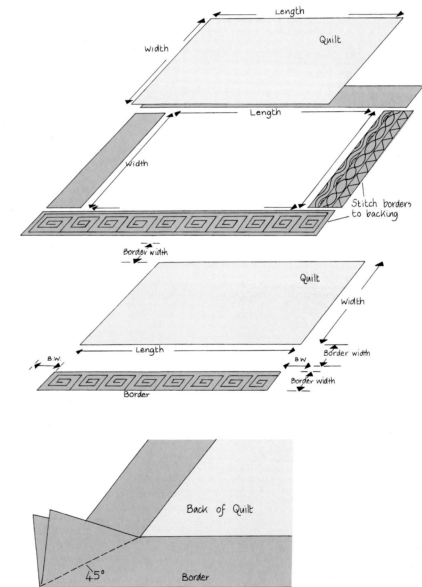

The design elements of The Gardenia Guardian, *a framed panel by Paddy Killer, are worked in free machine embroidery. The frame, which was made from scraps of frame mouldings, was painted to complement the main embroidery. Size: 40 cm × 45 cm (16 in × 18 in).*

Many embroideries are greatly enhanced by a sympathetic choice of frame and mount. Hardboard is used for a backing, while a matt creates a window for the work. To judge how much of the embroidery should be exposed and how wide the borders should be, take two L-shaped pieces of paper, cut to different widths and from different colours, both complementary to the embroidery. Lay these on the work to give you some idea of how it might look when framed.

Cut the hardboard to the size of the embroidery with borders, and cut the matt to the same size, with a window for the embroidery. Try to avoid square matts – rectangular ones are generally more effective, and it is in most cases more aesthetically pleasing if the bottom border is slightly deeper than the others. The embroidery is laced over the hardboard and the matt laid on top, ready for framing. The width of the frame should suit the work, and the frame, matt and embroidery should be seen as a single composition. If the mounted work is too shallow for the frame, it can be raised by laying narrow strips of cardboard along the edges, or by placing wedges at the corners. Always cover the back and seal it with tape to exclude dust and insects.

THE HAPPY ENDINGS

E mbroideries and quilts do not necessarily need to be framed or finished with precise, straight edges. In fact, unfinished fabric edges can provide a satisfying element.

LINING QUILTS AND EMBROIDERIES

A lining protects the back of the work and makes it look well finished. The lining fabric can be anything from a curtain lining fabric to a fabric similar to that used on the front of the work. To avoid uneven hanging, ensure that the grains of the front and lining fabrics run in the same direction. The edges of a soft hanging may be turned under, and the lining should be cut slightly smaller than the work, turned under, and slipstitched to the turned front.

LINING SOFT WALL PANELS AND QUILTS

Lining can be applied and used to edge the front of the work in a single operation. For this method, cut the lining fabric larger than the work, allowing an excess for the amount of border to show on the front. The border may be narrow or wide, depending on individual preference and design. This method works best on items no larger than quilts of single-bed size.

Lay the lining, cut to size, over the back of the work, checking that the grain lines match. Secure the lining to the back with rows of lockstitch, worked about 30cm (12in) apart. Fold the edges over to the front and pin them in place. Roll the raw edge under and slipstitch the edge by hand to the front side.

SINGLE STRIP EDGING

This is a useful finish for either soft wall hangings or quilts. With wrong sides together, pin a lining to the back of the work. Both front and lining should be the same size. Stitch around the perimeter of the piece to hold the fabrics in place. Cut binding strips from the selected edging fabric, being sure to cut them along the length of the grain. Stitch ends together to form a strip long enough to go all the way around the piece. Turn in the edges and press, as in commercially available bias binding tape.

Starting from the back of the work, pin the strip into place and stitch. Turn the piece to the front and, again, pin and baste into place, covering any stitching that may show on the edge. The edging may be attached by machine or by hand. Corners can also be mitred.

TIPS ON CARING FOR YOUR WORK

Never hang your work in direct sunlight or other intense light sources, nor over direct heat.

It is difficult to prevent dust from accumulating on hanging articles. Remove loose dust and lint with a duster, using a light touch. Textiles can be vacuum cleaned – use lower power – but any article that has loose or applied pieces should have a screen or net laid over it before you vacuum.

I find that a special-purpose bag, made for the article, is a handy way of storing and protecting embroideries. The bag may be quilted, with added padding to protect delicate items. Touch-and-close fastenings are easy to use.

QUILT CARE

The best place to store a quilt is on a bed. If a quilt must be stored elsewhere, try folding or rolling it, avoiding folds along lines of heavy stitching. Place acid-free tissue paper between folds and open and refold the quilt from time to time. Cardboard carpet or textile rolls are handy to roll quilts upon, as are plastic drain pipes. The larger the diameter of the roll, the better for the quilt. Quilts that have been made from fabrics that are colour-fast, or from your own dyed fabrics, if these have been properly set, will usually tolerate washing. Do not machine wash unless they have been designed to accept this kind of treatment. Wash quilts in a bathtub or other large receptacle in a tepid (preferably soft-water) solution, using mild soap. Rinse thoroughly and lay them flat to dry on absorbent material, such as towelling. Pat dry, and change towels as they get wet.

SUPPLIERS

In some cases, brand names of specific dyes have been mentioned. If you have any difficulty in obtaining these in your area, the manufacturers will be able to suggest sources of supply. Addresses are given below.

AUSTRALIA

Deka, The Spinning Parlour, Mrs Val Campbell, 15 Russel Street, Toowoomba 4350

Dylon, Jackel International Ltd, Jackel House, 32 South Street, Rydal Mere, NSW 216

Pebeo, Francheville Pty Ltd, No 1 to 5 Perry Street, Collingwood, Victoria 3066

BRITAIN

Deka, George Weil and Sons Ltd, 18 Hanson Street, London W1P 7DB

Dylon International Ltd, Worsley Bridge Road, Lower Sydenham, London SE26 5HD

Pebeo, Art Graphique, Unit 2, Poulton Close, Dover, Kent CT17 0HL

CANADA

Deka – as United States

Dylon, Farquhar International Ltd, 937 Dillingham Road, Pickering, Ontario

Pebeo, Nationart Canada Inc, 341-11éme Ave S, Sherbrooke Quebec

UNITED STATES

Deka, Decart Inc. PO Box 309, Morrisville, VT 05661

Dylon USA, 117 Franklin Park Avenue, Youngsville, North Carolina, 27596

Pebeo, Nationart Inc/Pebeo, 220 Ballardvale Street, Wilmington MA 01872

NEW ZEALAND

Deka, CC G Industries Ltd, PO Box 9523, Newmarket, Auckland

Dylon, T.A. Macalister Ltd, Private Bag, Auckland

Pebeo – as Australia

INDEX

ACKNOWLEDGMENTS

Many people have contributed to the making of this book, and it would be impossible to thank each one individually, but I would like, first and foremost, to thank all the skilled quilt artists and embroiderers who spent many hours designing and producing the finished works for this book. I would also like to thank my students, former students, and Margaret Hall.

Thanks are also due to the team of people who assisted in the production of the book: Shirley Patton, editorial director; Polly Boyd, project editor; Diana Brinton, text editor; Bill Mason, designer, and Stewart Grant, photographer.

I am also very grateful to the following suppliers:

AST Research, for the loan of a colour computer.

Barn Yarns, Petersfield, UK, and Adele Bates supplied some wools and the stool for the Sleeping Beauty hearth stool.

Crimple Craft Ltd, Harrogate, UK, for loaning cotton fabrics for photography.

DMC Creative World Ltd, in Leicester, UK, for supplying a variety of threads, wools and canvases.

Deka Farben (West Germany), for supplying dyes and paints.

Digital Research, for the loan of Artline, computer graphics programme.

Dylon International Ltd, London, for dyes and paints.

Elna Sewing Machines (GB) Ltd, for the loan of an Elna Press.

Freudenberg Nonwovens Ltd (The Vilene Organization), UK, for continued generous supplies of vilene.

Fujitsu Europe Ltd, for the loan of dot matrix and laser printers, and scanner.

George Weil & Sons Ltd, London, for stretcher frames and silk fabric.

Hitachi Ltd, for the loan of a digitizing tablet.

Madeira Threads UK Ltd, and Sarah and Ian MacPherson, for supplying a generous quantity of machine and hand embroidery threads, both for my own work and for that of many contributors.

Micrografx, for the loan of Designer, computer graphics programme.

Morris and Ingram (London) Ltd, for a touch-up gun for use with fabric paints.

Perivale-Gütermann Ltd, UK, for quilting and silk threads.

Pfaff (Britain) Ltd, for their continued support in supplying sewing machines, needles and accessories.

Raphäel (MaxSauer Co.) France, for a range of paint brushes.

Sakar International Ltd, for Caran D'Ache Prismalo pencils and Neocolor II (UK).